# ADVENTISM+
## VOL. 01: ORIGINS

IN THE BEGINNING

# MARCOS TORRES

*Adventism+ Vol. 1. Softcover*

**Self-Published by Marcos D. Torres**

**ISBN:** 978-1-7636905-1-6

© **2024 The Story Church Project**

For permissions or information contact: pastormarcos@thestorychurchproject.com

**Cover Designed** by Andrew Caroll at, 42 Design

For more Adventist Missional Resources go to:

www.thestorychurchproject.com

# CONTENTS

# WORDS TO KNOW

### Postmodernism (1960s-1990s)

*Postmodernism was a cultural and philosophical movement that questioned the idea of objective truth and grand narratives. It argued that knowledge is fragmented, relative, and subject to interpretation. Think of it like a puzzle with many pieces that don't quite fit together. Postmodernism challenged traditional notions of identity, history, and reality.*

### Metamodernism (2000s-present)

*Metamodernism is a more recent movement that builds upon postmodernism. It acknowledges the fragmentation of postmodernism but seeks to rebuild and find new ways to connect the puzzle pieces. Metamodernism is about oscillating between different perspectives, embracing ambiguity, and finding meaning in the contradictions. It's like trying to solve the puzzle while recognizing that new pieces might be added or old ones might change shape.*

## Posthumanism (1990s-present)

*Posthumanism, in the transhuman sense, is a philosophical and cultural movement that explores what it means to be human in the face of rapid technological advancements. It considers the potential for humans to merge with machines, overcome biological limitations, and become something more than just human. Think of it like upgrading your smartphone to a newer model – but instead, it's your own body and mind.*

## Missiology (Christian context, various time frames)

*Missiology is the study of Christian missionary work and the spread of Christianity. It examines the strategies, methods, and cultural contexts of sharing the Christian message. Missiology is like mapping out a journey to share a specific message with people from different backgrounds and cultures.*

## Contextualization (various time frames)

*Contextualization is the process of adapting a message, idea, or practice to a specific cultural, social, or historical context. It's like translating a book into a different language to make it more accessible to a new audience. Contextualization aims to make the message more relatable and relevant to the target audience.*

# INTRODUCTION

*"The church that is married to the spirit of this age,
becomes a widow in the next."*
**– William Ralph Inge**

They said we Adventists are always 20 years behind everyone else.

And then they laughed.

I laughed too.

And why not? It was true after all. Our church started discussing the impact of postmodernism on western society in the early 2000's. You'd think, by the way we talked about it, that it was some new, emerging phenomenon.

But the truth is post-modernism began in the 1950's and was at its height in the 60's and 70's. By the 1980's academics were already declaring its death. Fast forward another 20 years, and the SDA's were finally joining the conversation. Only, the conversation was by-and-large already over.

The world had moved on.

So, when they (the Adventist church members I was having potluck with) quipped about how tone-deaf we tend to be as a denomination, I had two choices: cry or laugh.

I chose to laugh in that moment. The crying came later.

Because this cultural detachment can only mean two things. First, that the world we exist in doesn't exist outside of our churches. Second, because we exist in no-longer-existent time capsules, we cannot effectively disciple the age we actually inhabit.

And that hurts. It hurts because this is our time. We are here now. You inhabit this moment, this limited space in time. The 1950's do not belong to us. Neither do the 1980's or even 1990's for that matter.

What belongs to us is the here and now. We are its inhabitants. We belong to these moments.

And yet, we are not present. We are not engaged. We are not connected. We live in containers of by gone eras. And in doing so, we answer questions people are no longer asking and express ourselves in language people no longer understand. We have become, in the words of Rabbi Abraham Joshua Heschel, "irrelevant, dull, oppressive, insipid."

A new cultural zeitgeist had been emerging for the past decade. And we were so out-of-touch, so detached from the world around us that we had no idea what this new zeitgeist was. With the death of postmodernism arrived the advent of meta-modernity. This metamodern mood is the prevailing milieu of our day. And soon, within the next 30 years, it will evolve and perhaps even pass away with the arrival of technological revolutions so radical, so impactful, and so breathtaking they will redefine society as a whole.

Like the agricultural revolution that forever changed the world, allowing our species to build empires.

Like the industrial revolution, that changed our empires forever, allowing an age of mass production, consumption, and comfort.

Like the digital revolution, that changed our industries forever, allowing an age of hyper-interconnectedness and the amplification of individualistic consumer culture.

There dawns upon us a new age where Artificial Intelligence will forever alter the course of human culture, redefining not just what it means to be a society, a nation, or a citizen — but what it means to be human altogether.

These changes are not science fiction, they are not wishful thinking, and they are not projected to take place after the next 100 years.

These changes are already here, all around us. And they are projected to radically alter the course of human history beginning in the next 5-10 years.

The world is headed toward the age of the cyborg and all the while, Adventists are still debating coffee. Something has to change.

In Adventism+ Volumes 1-4 my goal is to be a part of that change. Not to lead it or activate it because it's already happening. My goal here is simply to engage with it. To fan the flames the Spirit has already ignited. Because if we truly believe we have something beautiful to tell the world, we cannot afford to be out of touch anymore.

The changes that are coming are rapid ones. And big ones.

We cannot ride in the background, whispering among ourselves. We must find our voice and use it in ways that challenge and inspire the trajectory of modern humanity's pursuits.

And that's what Adventism+ will aim to do (in its own small and unique way).

## How will this book work?

First, let me tell you what this book is NOT. This book is not a nerdy exploration of every technological advancement being promoted at Silicon Valley. We are not going to wind through every rabbit trail the media and technological futurists throw at us. We are not going to become experts in gene editing, artificial intelligence, robotics, or cities in space.

Yes, we will mention these things. But the real focus of this book is to empower missional engagement. So, if you are looking for a nerdy book that pontificates on every tech trend imaginable while offering scholarly reflections that the average believer can barely comprehend, then this is not your book.

In fact, in this series we are not even going to focus exclusively on the future or invest tons of energy in painting a speculative image of what the year 2080 might look like. Instead, we are going to spend most of our time in the present. We will anchor our roots deep in the moment we inhabit and in doing so, engineer the necessary adaptive quotient for whatever the future might bring.

Yes, we will talk about the technological revolution and its implications for mission in the next few decades. But my goal is to do this as practically as possible, equipping and empowering us with tangible and useful insights that can actually move the needle on local church community engagement and mission.

So, if you were expecting a tantalizing set of books full of futuristic conjecture and sci-fi theology – I am sorry to disappoint. But if you are looking for a practical tool to help you understand our current metamodern milieu while anchoring you with the needed tools to become adaptive in the face of our rapidly evolving, techno-driven world. Then welcome to volume 1 of this 4-volume series.

In this first volume, here is what we are going to do:

1. Beginning with our current cultural reality (the secular, Metamodern age we inhabit) we will explore how our doctrinal articulations fail to speak to the language of the heart by addressing anxieties no longer present in contemporary cultural consciousness. This exploration of contemporary secular metamodernism will form the foundation of this entire 4 volume set. What this means is, this book will not explore the future in isolation to the present. The "here" will inform the "there."

2. From that foundation of "present" and "here", we will then be poised to adequately consider and address the coming technological revolution (AI, the singularity, and more) that is set to forever metamorph the human experience. Here, we will explore the changes and contextualization needed to keep our message fresh, relevant, and meaningful without compromising the inherent anti-conformist oddities that make it what it is.

Remember, the aim of this book is not to explore every possible angle and rabbit trail that relates to meta and post-human cultural shifts. That would be both impossible and way too nerdy (nerdier than this work already is).

Instead, my aim is a lot simpler. To interact and listen to the culture so that we can learn to articulate according to its own language. We do not want to wed the culture, for as the Anglican priest William Ralph Inge once said, "The church that is married to the spirit of this age, becomes a widow in the next."

But we do want to know it. To understand it. To appreciate it.

All with a simple vision. To no longer be the people who are always 20 years behind.

Because this is our time. This is our moment. It belongs to us, and we belong to it.

# 1

# EXPLORING METAMODERNISM & THE CONTEMPORARY SECULAR MIND

*"It is impossible to imagine a post-human missiology if we do not first understand the post to metamodern age we currently inhabit. To immerse ourselves in the study of our 'here' is the first step in engineering a foundation for our 'there'."*

Chapter 1:

# ORIGINS

---

*"Meaningless! Meaningless! . . . Utterly meaningless!*
*Everything is meaningless."*
**– The Preacher, Ecclesiastes 1:2 NIV**

Over the years, I have developed a passion and desire to reach those whom the church fails to reach most often—the secular, western individual. I have read and written blogs and books on the topic, delivered sermons, engaged with experts, been interviewed by others, and am currently involved in a new church specifically designed to reach a post-church society. Through this journey, I have learned to recognize how I push people away from God. And consequently, I have begun to identify how we collectively do the same.

One particular error stands out above the rest. The error is simple: in our attempts to reach the culture with the gospel, we have begun, perhaps unintentionally, to see the post-church mind as a *problem*. When we see the culture as a problem, people become projects instead of people. The secular mind thus becomes a quandary to be resolved—an obstacle, hurdle, dilemma, and nuisance which we, as the church, must fix—an impenetrable fortress that, rather than admire, we inspect with the hopes of finding a crevice we can exploit to gain entry.

In reaction to this damaging posture, I have begun asking: What if the culture's aversion to Christianity wasn't so much a problem as an opportunity? What if we slowed down and stopped trying to find the key or the secret to reach the culture, and instead sat down with it, inhaled its fragrance, appreciated its questions, felt its despair, and learned to sing its songs, speak its language, and dance according to its rhythm? What if, by admiring the fortress with genuine sincerity and authenticity, it's gates let us in?

In this approach, the mind of the secular is—to appropriate the words of Danish philosopher Søren Kierkegaard—no longer "a problem to be solved but a reality to be experienced." I enter into a relationship with this mind and learn to listen to it, observe its color, and taste its flavors. I am not obsessed with proving it wrong or with stamping my ideological convictions onto it so that the "contact" emerges as a mere parrot of Adventist orthodoxy. Instead, I am searching to experience life with this mind, to belong, and to explore together. In the context of this mutual dance, I have discovered, Jesus shines brightest.

But some repeatedly inquire: Why approach the secular mind this way? What is wrong with the traditional doctrinal approach Adventists have been mastering for decades? What is so bad about just preaching the old truths, proclaiming the straight testimony, sounding the midnight cry or telling the old, old story?

## The Absurdity of Life

To answer this question, I want to take a few moments to explore, the transition, from the sincere naïveté (faith, hope, and certainty) that we, as believers, experience to the fragmented ambivalence (cynicism, nihilism, relativism) present in the culture.

Now, this is no easy task. One of the most sobering thoughts I have had to meditate on as I invest in reaching the culture is this: *I do not know, nor have I ever known, what it is like to live in a state of fragmented ambivalence.* I was brought up in an Adventist home and taught to trust God from my birth. Consequently, I have always had an enthusiastic lens through which to perceive my being and its place in reality. I simply don't know what it's like to exist without this foundation.

What this means at the practical level is that there is a huge chasm separating my experience as a human being and that of the modern secular mind immersed in fragmented ambivalence. This state of immersion is best described in the words of Gary Nelson, in his Huffington Post article, "Getting Churchy in a Time of Chaos and Hate: A Personal Journey" when he noted that this state of fragmentation is one in which comfort is "elusive" and "fleeting"—an experience in which even sleep itself becomes a "dance with the unwelcome strangers."[1]

And this state of being is not reserved for a few hyper-introspective individuals but for the whole of modern society. Research shows that an increasing number of people are born into and raised in non-faith environments, never experiencing the enthusiastic expectation derived from faith in a good and loving God.[2] Thus, emerging generations are left to manufacture and construct meaning out of the chaos, navigating the task of justifying their existence against the absurdity of life on their own.

And just what is this absurdity of life? Before I answer this question, allow me to make a very significant statement. If the promise of redemption is the field in which the believer sows his identity and hope, the absurdity of life—replete with its inherent fragmentation and ambivalence—is the field in which the secular man attempts to sow his purpose. This is the differentiating understructure between people of faith and people of no faith. Therefore, understanding the absurdity of life is essential for those of us who aspire to engage with the culture. Failing to comprehend this means, we will never be capable of interacting meaningfully with the secular mind.

So what is this absurdity of life? In a non-faith world, this phrase summarizes a fundamental and assumed premise: *that life is absurd*. From start to finish, it is a dance with the incongruous, with mild glimpses of cohesion. What are we as humans meant to do with this absurdity? When a parent buries a child, there is no rational explanation. When a marriage ends in divorce, we witness the death of what was once entered into, starry-eyed and magical, and it is absurd (enough to convince younger generations from marrying[3]). And how are we to confront death and disease—when what was once fully conscious now ceases to exist as though it had never been— how nonsensical! How do we make sense of injustice, addiction, massacres, and their inherent idiocy? What about depression, anxiety, phobias and dark pathologies that ebb and flow within each of us? Or of the dystopian future to which we all seem to be heading?

But bizarre as these scenarios may be, they do not, in and of themselves, exhaust the absurdity that a fragmented culture is contending with. Instead, the best way to fully appreciate this absurdity is through the Greek Myth of Sisyphus, as popularly analyzed by the existentialist Albert Camus.[4]

## Sisyphus and Meaninglessness

The myth of Sisyphus goes something like this: Having angered the gods, the king of Corinth (Sisyphus) was condemned to the eternal task of rolling a large boulder to the top of a hill, only for the boulder to roll back to the bottom every time it reached the peak. Over and over again, Sisyphus repeats the task with no end in sight. The most painful part of the story, Camus observes, is that Sisyphus is not simply condemned to an eternal task, but to an eternal *meaningless* task. That is, all of his effort, all of his labor, all of his sweat and blood and agony ultimately amount to nothing.

This myth captures the heart of non-faith culture with stunning clarity. Life, in this portrait, appears to be a pointless and senseless struggle where we fight to our last breath to validate our existence only to die and be forgotten. You will suffer in life. You will be a victim in life. You will weep—not the surface romantic tragedy but the soul crushing tears flowing from fountains of repressed agony. You will do your best, pursue your dreams, and build your empire, only for life to mock you with the seeming emptiness and vanity of it all. And yet, at the same time, "the body shrinks from annihilation"[5] as though it wants to go on to something better somewhere beyond. It is this experience, this "wresting meaning from reality"[6], this thing we all must endure for no apparent reason, that can only be described as absurd. Absurd because deep within there is something that cries out for meaning, and yet, to the naked eye, the universe is indifferent to our longings. The infinite blackness mocks us and reminds us that we are insignificant, that all things are inconsequential, and that even our greatest and most brilliant achievements are absolutely inconsequential. The preacher affirmed this perspective, when he declared, "Meaningless! Meaningless!

. . . Utterly meaningless! Everything is meaningless" (Ecclesiastes 1:2). Ellen White echoed this thought when she wrote, "[Men] often they think they are plucking fruit most essential [but] they find it altogether . . . nothingness."[7] And the British theologian Adam Clarke paraphrased the preacher in melodious poetry, declaring:

O vain, deluding world! Whose largest gifts

Thine emptiness betray, like painted clouds,

Or watery bubbles: as the vapor flies,

Dispersed by lightest blast, so fleet thy joys,

And leave no trace behind.[8]

This Sisyphus and his eternal meaninglessness is an archetype of the thought that permeates our culture's substrate. From the scientist who declares that our universe—like Clarke's "painted clouds" and "vapor"—will die in due time, and all memory that we are will be erased, to the executive who drags his feet through life—a mindless zombie, animated but not living—most people today, declared the holocaust survivor and psychologist Viktor Frankl "have the means to live but no meaning to live for."[9] Thus, the culture that surrounds our churches, with all of its amusements and pleasures, cannot escape its reality—it is drowning in absurdity.

When confronted with this absurdity, humankind must do something. There must be an objective to which we can aspire to go on living. Something meaningful enough to justify the futility of it all. Sisyphus must find some means through which to avoid insanity. If he is to live with some measure of happiness, then what is he to do, condemned to eternal vanity?

## Amusement

For some, the pursuit of meaning is sought through amusement. They spend their lives partying, indulging in depravity and embracing hedonism. These individuals, while, pushing the giant boulder up the hill, attempt to numb the meaninglessness of life through materialism, entertainment, and the pursuit of pleasure. For some, it's sex, cheap novels and pornography. Alcohol, gambling and drugs. Yet another crowd seeks the accumulation of temporal goods and experiences—anything to distract the mind—to medicate it against the absurdity of life. On the surface, they appear full of joy and excitement. Underneath, in the depths/recesses of the soul, there is a festering gash. This sentiment is best captured in John Mayer's ballad "Something's Missing" when he asked, "How come everything I think I need, always comes with batteries? What do you think it means?"

Ultimately, the system fails, for the way of the amused is but a knocking at the door of significance. Thus, the twentieth-century Scottish writer Bruce Marshal could assert, "Every man who knocks on the door of a brothel is looking for God."[10]

## Duties

For others, the pursuit of meaning is found through duty. They invest their lives in the responsibilities of work, career, financial success and familial commitments. These individuals fully dedicate themselves to the pursuit of accomplishment, discipline, positive thinking, and systems. They excel in their jobs, get awards, earn PhDs, and lead a strict, ethical lives. Such people cannot fathom the foolishness of those who pursue amusement, often seeing them as wasted potential and judging them for their perceived stupidity. However, what the duty-bound fail to realize is how similar they are to those who chase pleasure. Both are pushing a giant boulder up a hill for no apparent reason, only to have it roll back down again. They are repeating the same futile chapter, only worse than Sisyphus's, for they are aware of their mortality and the limited time they have left. With each passing day, the grave draws nearer, they are left to wonder, and "To what end?" Consequently, both suffer, grappling with the incongruity of a soul yearning for meaning against an indifferent reality that suggests that none exists. Although their approaches may differ, their goal is the same and both, eventually, find themselves either profoundly unsatisfied at best or irreparably broken at worst.

## Transcendence

For others still, the absurdity of life is mitigated through transcendence. They find, meaning in a spectrum of ideals, from the liturgy of traditional religion to the free spirited adventure of self-defined spirituality. For them, the pain of reality is transcended, as pain and suffering do not matter in the presence of a greater beyond. They often attempt to justify life's pain with platitudes of an afterlife, framing it as preparation for a future elevation into a greater dimension of existence—a heaven in which all true meaning ultimately resides. Thus, their lives are dedicated to the transcendent and whatever rituals and paths must be followed to escape the state of absurdity. It was to such people that Karl Marx referred when he declared religion to be "the opiate of the masses," masking the pain of reality by promising a pie in the sky in which all our hopes are placed, yet saying and doing nothing about the real, day-to-day absurdity that must still be faced.

Regardless of the approach one takes, or if they oscillate between two or all three, the experience remains the same. People are trying to find a reason to justify going on in the face of a hollow, sterile and empty existence. They are fighting for a reason: to get out of bed in the morning, for a skip in their step, or for a purpose that animates their being. Post-modernity may in fact be an ironic and dark vision of the future. Still, the philosophy fails to address the real experience of life that calls humans, regardless of creed, to pursue enthusiasm and the tenuous "better" that lies somewhere beyond. As a result, the culture is increasingly now moving toward meta-modernity—a new approach to existence that attempts to embrace enthusiasm while still believing that the future is empty. Thus, rather than trying to fight it, the absurdity is increasingly embraced as a natural part of life. This is a fancy way of saying that the culture is settling in meaninglessness and hopelessness as the natural state of things. There is no use fighting it; just accept it and try and manufacture some sense of meaning in it, for the eighty years will soon pass away and eventually all memories of us, and yet we press on. To what end? We don't know—only that we do.

In the midst of this experience, of balancing the chaos of being with the impulse for the beyond, the culture finds itself in absurdity. Most tragic to the one who comprehends this is thus the traditional Adventist dialectic. The Adventist arrives with conviction, declaring: "The Sabbath is not on the 1st day of the week, but the 7th!" She continues, "Why so many denominations, you ask?" (No, I didn't) "Did you know ghosts are not real? That the only true church is the Seventh-day Adventist remnant? That archeology proves the Bible is true? That evolution is false? Oh, and while we are at it, get a load of who the 'little horn' is and the Antichrist and the mark of the beast! And by the way, jewelry is bad, and tattoos, and Hollywood, and syncopated beats."

Oh I know, not all Adventists articulate our message in such a stringent framework. But for those of us who resist these more toxic angles, we rarely have a meaningful alternative. And the end result is a movement that devolves into petty bickering, fighting about things that don't really matter all the while thinking we are doing somebody a favor. But the truth is, the culture we are meant to companion does not even notice our skirmishes. The things we find so obscenely interesting, the endless asinine squabbles, the "oh so important" topics which we fight and scream about, the ones we allow to divide and distract us—no one really cares about them. And I pray the irony does not elude you—that a people with the antidote to absurdity, with a real answer to the suffering of being, to the hearts cry for meaning and significance, with something truly valuable to offer a generation suffocating in chaos—that we would be so distracted and obsessed with the drivel of religiosity. That we would be so out of touch with the heart of the lost. That we would be preaching a message that no one is listening to, all the while thinking we are faithful to the call. What are we to do with such irony? The irony of a people with hope but distracted by nonsense, while a culture without hope passes by, and doesn't notice we are here.

Ellen White once wrote, "Christ bids you look to him as the Illuminator of your darkened souls."[11] In this little statement lies a profound revelation: the upside-down we all contend against is not to be medicated via amusements, duties, or religion but to be navigated in a relationship. There is, in fact, a completely different way of interacting with the absurdity that invites us into an intimate and personal encounter with the one who can illuminate the darkness and provide us with everything our hearts are searching for because, in truth, these hearts were made for intimacy with him. In this vision, we are not hiding from the chaos but rather confronting it—not alone, but in relationship with the one who brings order out of absurdity. To this end, CS Lewis famously stated, "If I find in myself a desire which no experience in this world can satisfy, the most probable explanation is that I was made for another world."

If we want to keep having this conversation about reaching the secular mind, we must first learn to sit with its lament and its perceived escapes from such despair (amusement, duties, and transcendence). Because the unconventional truth is that despite the angst, the culture is generally happy. The perceived escapes are working for many. They go through life empty, thinking they are full. They live each day with expectation, despite the fact that they have nothing to expect. The culture, despite its absurdity, is not miserable and collapsing. It is far too distracted for that—too amused, too occupied and too abstracted by its perceived escapes. And the church's message is hardly even noticed.

Thus, we must learn to understand this angst and its escapes and aim to interact meaningfully with them. We must set aside the argumentation and sermonizing that say nothing to this collective experience and instead explore the biblical invitation to redemption. As we navigate the mind of the culture and learn to appreciate it, we will be able to see just how trite the message we often proclaim is in the eyes of those we have been called to reach. We will discover that for too long, we have been preaching to ourselves about ourselves, all the while thinking we are preaching to others. Only then will we be capable of re-imagining our message and mining from it treasure that speaks to the existential sorrow of the age.

# NOTES

[1]   Nelson, Gary. "Getting Churchy in a Time of Chaos and Hate: A Personal Journey." HuffPost. Accessed [date]. https://www.huffpost.com/entry/getting-churchy-in-a-time-of-chaos-and-hate_b_1551423.

[2 ]  Lipka, Michael. "A Closer Look at America's Rapidly Growing Religious 'Nones.'" Pew Research Center. Accessed [date]. https://www.pewresearch.org/fact-tank/2015/05/13/a-closer-look-at-americas-rapidly-growing-religious-nones/.

[3]   Mintz, Steven. "Is Marriage in Decline? The Percentage of Unmarried Americans Is Approaching an All-Time High. But Why?" Psychology Today. Accessed [date]. https://www.psychologytoday.com/au/blog/the-prime-life/201503/is-marriage-in-decline.

[4]   Camus, Albert. "The Myth of Sisyphus and Other Essays." Amazon. Accessed [date]. https://www.amazon.com/exec/obidos/ASIN/0679733736/braipick-20.

[5]   Popova, Maria. "Albert Camus on the Will to Live and the Most Important Question of Existence." Brain Pickings. Accessed [date]. https://www.brainpickings.org/2016/11/07/camus-myth-of-sisyphus-suicide/.

[6]   Popova, Maria. "Alan Watts on the Antidote to the Loneliness of the Divided Mind, Our Integration with the Universe, and How We Wrest Meaning from Reality." Brain Pickings. Accessed [date]. https://www.brainpickings.org/2016/11/01/alan-watts-wisdom-of-insecurity-3.

[7]   White, Ellen G. "This Day with God." p. 169.

[8]   Clarke, Adam. Bible Commentary. Accessed [date]. https://bibletools.info.

[9]   Frankl, Viktor. "Man's Search for Meaning." Amazon. Accessed [date]. https://www.amazon.com/Mans-Search-Meaning-Viktor-Frankl/dp/0807014273.

Notes

[10] Marshall, Bruce. "The World, the Flesh and Father Smith." Amazon. Accessed [date]. https://www.amazon.com/The-World-Flesh-Father-Smith/dp/B001V674RE.

[11] White, Ellen G. "This Day with God." p. 169.

Chapter 2:

# ABSURDITY

---

*"Fundamentalists live life with an exclamation point.*
*I prefer to live my life with a question mark."*
**–Amos Oz**

The state of absurdity (the tension between meaninglessness and meaning) is a very real experience that must be understood and appreciated by Adventists if we wish to develop a meaningful approach to evangelism in the secular sphere. It's not simply that people disagree with our doctrines, frameworks or propositions; rather, the self of the post-everything mind is sown in a field so divergent from what the believer knows that it develops an entirely different approach to life. Consequently, most people turn to either amusement, the duties of life, or transcendence in order to deal with the absurdity that this tension creates.

In this scenario, church and spirituality become meaningful only when the chosen system (amusement, duty, or transcendence) collapses. For example, the amused discovers pain in his pleasure after the novelty of said pleasure wears off. The musical artist Famba captures this experience best when he sang, "I've been searching for salvation in a bottle, but I ain't found nothing there but misery."[1]

Similarly, the man of duty finds himself dissatisfied and lost in passionless ethics, leading him to the classic "midlife crisis" in which he attempts to recover some sense of what is wild and unscripted in life—an experience so common in the West that in 1965, Roger Daltrey of "The Who" sang the timeless line, "things they look so awful cold, I hope I die before I get old."[2]

Meanwhile, the transcendent one finds that, despite his philosophy and mystical platitudes, life's suffering overwhelms him nonetheless, and he cannot escape its agony—an experience that has, in part—given birth to what Jean-François Lyotard described as the postmodern "incredulity toward metanarratives."[3]

It's often at these junctures in life that people will become open to exploring God. However, while they are open to exploration, this in no way means that the language Adventists speak will make any sense to them. This is because a mind sown in absurdity speaks a completely different language to a mind sown in faith. Thus, we cannot assume that once a person becomes open to God or embraces the reality of God's existence, they are automatically ready to consume traditional Adventist frameworks. Quite the opposite is true. In this scenario, the secular man approximates the pond of Adventist thought and, driven by a desire to explore the metaphysical, dips his toes in the water. If he is met by fundamentalism, simplistic ideas, or irrelevant concepts framed in a language he does not comprehend, he retreats. Sadly, our traditional evangelistic approach fuels this sort of repulsive experience. Therefore, to begin drafting a new and more effective approach, we need to rethink our entire paradigm, and I contend that this reimagining must begin at the level of truth.

## Truth and the Absurdity of Life

One of the underlying presuppositions in Adventist evangelism is that we possess the truth, which we believe is something every soul needs to encounter to experience salvation Of course, this position is both logical and biblical. However, we get into trouble when we assume that the culture views truth the same way we do, essentially believing that our attitudes about "truth" are universally shared. In reality, the truth is far more complicated.

To begin with, human beings tend, to speak two different languages. The first I refer to as "conceptual language" which simply means the words, colloquialisms and terminology we use to express concepts. The second I call "soul language" or "the language of being." This second language is deeper, as it is the language our heart speaks, revolving more around our moods and emotions. For example, a man can say he loves his wife, but if pushed for a reason why, he eventually gets frustrated and says, "I don't know, I just do!" This scenario demonstrates the limitations of conceptual language in fully capturing the depth and complexity of the language of being. The language of being is much deeper and cannot always be articulated through mere words or phrases. Another example is a pastor who tries to copy the words and fashion of the youth in order to "relate" to them. Most young people see this as a gimmick, and it doesn't generally work. However, most of us have seen that older gentleman who is anything but "cool," and yet the youth love him. Why is that? It's because this man has mastered the art of speaking to them on a deeper level, transcending superficial styles. Through authentic relationship, he taps into the emotions and experiences of a new generation.

It's important to recognize these two levels of language to connect meaningfully with the culture. Returning to the concept of truth, we can see that the typical Adventist has a conceptual approach to truth, but also a "soul language" about it. At the conceptual level, truth is a very simple concept. That which is true is, well, true. It stands in contrast to that which is false. It's black and white, right and wrong, up and down. Truth is factual, self-evident and absolute. At the level of "soul" language, though, truth is more than just an academic concept; but an enthusiastic idea, a treasure worth pursuing—to know it is to taste freedom from the oppression of lies. All of this results in an enthusiastic, sincere mood that shapes how Adventists see and express the concept of "truth."

However, the contemporary culture lacks the same connection to truth, both conceptually and spiritually. Conceptually speaking, that which is true cannot be contrasted with that which is false, for both can be true and false at the same time. Thus, British playwright Harold Pinter could say:

> There are no hard distinctions between what is real and what is unreal, nor between what is true and what is false. A thing is not necessarily either true or false; it can be both true and false.[4]

For the secular mind, therefore, truth—if it even exists—is more gray than black and white, and encompasses various shades as well. It is not as simple as right and wrong, as context alters the relationship of things, meaning what is right for you may be wrong for me, and vice versa. A distinction exists between "facts" which we can all affirm as a shared perspective because it is objective (like the White House is in Washington, D.C.) and "truth," which cannot be affirmed as a shared perspective because it is subjective (like Jesus is *the* savior). Thus, the concept of truth—whatever it may be—is neither self-evident nor absolute. To know truth is to know *your* truth, and thus to taste *your* freedom from *your* lies. However, your truth and freedom are personal to *you*, meaning that if applied to me, the same truth that has liberated you could oppress me.

That last line deserves more exploration, for it reveals that there is more to the culture's relationship with truth than the basic conceptual relativism we often boil it down to. For the culture, truth is not simply a non-thing but a frightening thing. For some, absolute truth lies at the foundation of every injustice, from racial oppression to sexual orientation and gender discrimination. For many others, the very concept of an absolute truth, even if divorced from injustice, lacks finesse and beauty. The postmodern philosopher Jean Baudrillard encapsulated this perfectly when he noted:

> Postmodernity is said to be a culture of fragmentary sensations, eclectic nostalgia, disposable simulacra, and promiscuous superficiality, in which the traditionally valued qualities of depth, coherence, meaning, originality, and authenticity are evacuated or dissolved amid the random swirl of empty signals.[5]

And these "random" and "empty signals"—this experience of "fragmentation," "disposability," "evacuation," and "dissolution"—are seen as beautiful, something to be celebrated not repaired. Thus, it's imperative to understand as Adventists that this perspective of truth is not necessarily something the secular man finds troublesome. At the level of "soul" language, no truth is liberating! French philosopher Jean-Paul Sartre surmised it best when he penned, "no meaning is relief."[6]

Thus, in the secular *vision du monde*, there is no absolute truth, no clear purpose for existence, and this, rather than being terrifying, actually sets me free to determine my own truth and my own direction. This means that I can live my life with total autonomy. There is no religious figure restraining my impulses, no ancient text controlling my ambitions, and no communal social conventions that forcefully mold my life. Best of all, there is no metaphysical judgment at which I am held to account. This is not some philosophical excuse for hedonism, as some Christians may argue, but rather an invitation to embrace absurdity, to dance with the meaninglessness and emptiness of it all, and to allow my life to become a work of art that creates meaning and beauty in a world of my own design.

This absence of truth offers the culture freedom from the oppression of the religious boundaries, which many believe have stifled humanity's progress and social evolution for too long. Thus, while the Adventist values truth, the secular mind either detests it at best or is indifferent to it at worst. Therefore, the absence of truth is not something to be lamented in the post-everything world; rather, it is something to be celebrated. At the level of soul language, truth represents freedom for the Adventist, but to the secular mind, freedom is found in the absence of truth. This leads the mind of the culture toward the fulfillment of what Gabriel Marcel described as "to rejoice in his own annihilation."[7]

## PERSPECTIVES ON TRUTH

|  | Mind of Faith | Mind of non-Faith |
|---|---|---|
| **Conceptual** | Truth is absolute, factual, self-evident | Truth is relative, distinction between facts and truth, not self-evident |
| **Language of Soul** | Truth is freedom<br>Lies are oppression | No truth is freedom<br>Truth is oppression |

With this divergence in our understanding of what constitutes truth, it becomes clear that the church is not only contending with its lack of relevance in an absurd world. It is also confronting a cathartic suspicion, loathing, and indifference toward truth. The end result of these divergent perspectives is collision.

Along comes the Adventist with the "truth" assuming the people around him share his enthusiastic appreciation of truth. But they don't. So the proclamation of truth, rather than reaching the hearts of the secular listeners, collides violently with the impregnable wall of incredulity that protects them from the thing they deem oppressive. Understanding this challenge must lead us to ask, how then can we approach the culture with the truth?

In order to set a foundation for exploring this question meaningfully, we need to examine two different approaches to truth and how they interact with the secular mind. To simplify matters, we will explore truth using the imagery of water in a stagnant state and a flow state.

### Truth as Stagnant

We've all encountered stagnant water bodies. Stagnant water is a breeding ground of bacteria and filth, something we naturally stay away from. In the same way that stagnant water repels us, stagnant truth repels the culture. By "stagnant" I mean truth that doesn't move. It is set, cannot be questioned, deconstructed, or modified.

Consequently, this perspective nurtures a culture of elitism and narcissism, where the believer sees himself and his/her community of faith as exclusively righteous. Seventh-day Adventists often succumb to this trap due to our high regard for the concept of truth. The end result in most cases is a culture of people who cannot engage meaningfully with anyone outside their own immediate community of faith. Their secular or non-Adventist friendships rapidly dissipate as they become the kinds of people who, in the words of Amos Oz, "live life with an exclamation point."[8]

To the contrary, and as cleverly summarized by Oz, the secular mind prefers to engage reality with a "question mark." Thus, even when such a person begins to explore God and faith, a person or church with a stagnant perspective on truth will speak a language of being that is far too intense, rigid and arrogant. In such scenarios, the Adventist fails to capitalize on the introspective season of the secular mind, instead repelling the seeker with an overly black-and-white vision of reality. This is because the secular mind sees the absence of truth as freedom and the presence of an absolute truth as oppressive. Thus, while open to faith, no man is ever open to oppression, preferring instead to remain in darkness despite its absurdity. For at least the darkness gifts the conscience with autonomy.

To connect with the culture, one must adopt a different approach to truth. This leads us to the concept of truth as flow.

**Truth as Flow**

Truth as stagnant has a number of problems, starting with the fact that it's simply not biblical. Instead, truth in scripture is presented as a progressive flow. This means that it has a simple starting place, a spring if you will, that then travels through time, culture, and seasons, bringing along new revelations and insights. Similar to a body of water flowing into the immensity of the ocean. This view of truth views truth as a process much like a small body of water flowing from a mountain top, down through time, and into an infinite ocean of reality. The truth-seeker in this scenario can be pictured as a man leaning over the current and scooping some freshwater in his hands to drink. The water being truth in motion toward an infinite ocean of truth where we, as temporal beings, can only ever consume small portions of it.

The practical outworking of this view is threefold. First, its proponents recognize that they don't know all truth, for while truth is absolute their grasp on said truth is only ever miniscule. They expect to learn more as time and seasons come and go. Second, they acknowledge their fallibility. For them, truth is absolute in the sense that it has a reliable ontological source (objectively absolute) but my personal understanding of that truth is constantly evolving. Third, not only, does its proponent expect to learn more truth as time advances, but they also expect to relearn the little of truth they already possess.

In other words, as God reveals more truth, they expect that new revelations will not simply agree with old ones, but that they will expand, enhance and clarify the truth they already possess. Ellen White captured this view of truth well when she wrote:

> "The truth of God is progressive; it is always onward, going from strength to a greater strength, from light to a greater light. We have every reason to believe that the Lord will send us increased truth, for a great work is yet to be done.

In our knowledge of truth, there is first a beginning in our understanding of it, then a progression, then completion; first the blade, then the ear, and after that the full corn in the ear. Much has been lost because our ministers and people have concluded that we have had all the truth essential for us as a people; but such a conclusion is erroneous and in harmony with the deceptions of Satan; for truth will be constantly unfolding." White, Ellen G: Sign of the Times, May 26, 1890.

This approach to truth, when embraced at the visceral level, generates an approach that is capable of journeying with the secular mind. We approach the seeker as fellow seekers, not as gurus. We acknowledge our limitations, our fallibility, and the fact that even our knowledge is but a tiny flow into a vast ocean of knowledge we have not even begun to scratch. Not only this, but we can admit that even what we do know is but a basic understanding of much bigger themes that time will unfold for us.

Thus, the threat of an absolute truth with its totalistic claims and oppression is calmed. The secular man knows that to pursue truth with this perspective means that wherever he goes there will be no compulsion, no coercion and no provocation. His conscience will retain its autonomy even when being challenged by meta-truths.

What this translates to is, even if there is an absolute truth, it is not oppressive and does not stake a coercive claim over individual conscience.

This is a truth perspective which the secular mind is more likely to engage with, for it interacts meaningfully with the language of its soul.

|  | Secular Mind | Result |
|---|---|---|
| **Truth as Stagnant** | Truth is oppressive meets truth is absolute, "I know it all" | Interpreted as a threat, Collision, Reluctance |
| **Truth as Flow** | Truth is oppressive meets truth is progressive, "I am seeking too" | Interpreted as safe, Awakens Curiosity, Willingness to explore |

And yet, all of this is about change. With the arrival of humanoid robots in mass production, augmented reality overlayed as holograms over the physical world, and an increasing dual-dimensional existence between what is real and what is digital, the struggle over what is true will eventually give way to a struggle over what is real. And if we have not yet learned how to speak to the heart of a culture at odds with truth, what hope do we have of connecting with a world questioning the very nature of reality itself?

## Conclusion

The above scenarios are more than the mere opinionated codification or observation of this one author. Rather, they flow from the very real experience of modern day people who interact with our evangelistic approach.

In their research project, "Millennial Perceptions of Adventist Public Evangelism" Dr. Allan Parker and Emily Charvat found that, despite a relatively positive experience and appreciation for Adventist evangelism, Millennials noted that "Adventists (74 percent), conspiracy theorists (57 percent), and Christians of other faiths (47 percent) are [most] likely to be attracted to evangelistic meetings based on the advertising."[9] However, when it comes to attracting "non-Christians" only 20 percent believed our approach effective, dropping to a mere 6 percent for Millennials.[10]

Furthermore, the majority of Millennials harbor negative perceptions of the advertising strategies employed, expressing reluctance to invite friends and deeming the approach outdated and irrelevant to their generation.[11][12] In other words, these evangelistic series are designed to speak to a bygone culture and generation that no longer exist. They make assumptions about their listeners that end up attracting everyone but the secular culture that surrounds us. It's not simply the clash in conceptual language that appears to drive these conclusions but the clash in language of being. Our approach is literally using a different language both at the level of concept and being and is, consequently, interpreted as a threat even by those who have entered a season of introspection and are open to seeking God.

Dr. Jesse Wilson summarized this best when he wrote:

> It's obvious why some evangelistic ideas and efforts are unfruitful. The calendar has changed, but the methods are the same. Going to the evangelistic campaign is like taking a nice stroll down memory lane.[13]

I couldn't agree more. Adventists exist at a point in tension that invites us to develop an evangelistic approach resonant with the soul of a culture that finds beauty in the absurdity of life. And it begins with adopting a perspective of truth as fluid, capable of interacting meaningfully with the secular mind. From that starting place, we will have the necessary insight and capacity to engage with a rapidly approaching generation that will subvert the very meaning of reality itself.

# NOTES

[1]  Famba. Lyrics to "Swear to God." © Ultra Tunes, Songtrust Ave.

[2]  The Who. Lyrics to "My Generation." © Universal Music Publishing Group.

[3]  Nasrullah Mambrol. "The Postmodern as 'Incredulity towards Metanarratives.'" Accessed [date]. https://literariness.org/2016/04/03/the-postmodern-as-the-incredulity-towards-metanarratives.

[4]  Harold Pinter. "Harold Pinter – Nobel Lecture." Accessed [date]. https://www.nobelprize.org/prizes/literature/2005/pinter/25621-harold-pinter-nobel-lecture-2005.

[5]  Jean Baudrillard. "Simulacra and Simulations." University of Michigan Press, 1994.

[6]  The School of Life. "Philosophy – Sartre." Accessed [date]. https://www.youtube.com/watch?v=3bQsZxDQgzU.

[7]  Wikipedia. "Gabriel Marcel." Accessed [date]. https://en.wikipedia.org/wiki/Gabriel_Marcel#cite_note-11.

[8]  Richard Reeder. "The Words and Wisdom of Amos Oz Live On." Accessed [date]. https://aliteraryreeder.wordpress.com/2018/12/29/the-words-and-wisdom-of-amos-oz-live-on.

[9 ]Allan Parker and Emily Charvat. "Millennial Perceptions of Adventist Public Evangelism." Slide 18. Accessed [date]. https://www.slideshare.net/parkersda/millennial-perceptions-of-adventist-public-evangelism.

[10] Ibid., Slide 20.

[11] Ibid., Slide 23.

[12] Ibid., Slide 51.

[13] Jesse Wilson. "How Adventist Evangelism Hurts Adventist Evangelism." Accessed [date]. https://drjessewilson.com/bad-evangelism.

CHAPTER 3:

# **ELASTICITY**

---

*"If we distance ourselves and our point of view, a
culture will always look peculiar to us."*
### *–Shahar Fisher*

We are nearly ready to begin re-imagining Adventism. So far, we have seen three very important points that call us to re-imagine our evangelistic approach. First, the secular mind is immersed in absurdity—an experience most people of faith are entirely unfamiliar with. When we fail to recognize this immense distinction, we perpetuate an evangelistic narrative that answers questions no one is asking (more on this below).

The second is that the absurdity of life is generally escaped via amusement, duties, or transcendence. These approaches were initially introduced (in a different framework) by the father of existentialism, Søren Kierkegaard, in what he referred to as "stages on life's way."[1] The idea here is that the secular heart is often only ready to engage biblical faith when the chosen method of navigation collapses. Nevertheless, even though the culture seeks to escape absurdity, it is simultaneously a thing to be celebrated, not lamented. Therefore, just because a person's navigation system has collapsed does not mean that they are suddenly open to consuming traditional Adventist orthodoxy. They would much rather return to the absurdity, for at least there is autonomy in it—a virtue absolute truth proposals threaten with annihilation.

This leads us to the third point: the secular person speaks a different language of being to the person of faith. When we fail to recognize these divergences, we foster a missional approach that essentially attracts people who are already sort of like us. Anyone in that narrow box is tragically excluded.

Each of these points are important to note if we wish to begin reimagining the way in which we share faith at a conceptual level and also at the level of being because, the truth is, our present system doesn't speak to the secular mind but rather to the religious.[2] As a result, most of our evangelistic campaigns and local church cultures attract the already religious and already conservative.[3] Very few secular people—especially those most impacted by postmodernity, walk through our doors, and even fewer stick around. The same is true of our Bible study resources, most of which are designed for people with some sort of traditional religious background. [4] To meet the culture where it is and companion it toward Christ, therefore, requires a contextualization that goes deeper than surface methodology and into the very heart of who we are.

In this book, I want to focus mostly on what we say because I believe that once we have contextualized our message to speak meaning to post- and meta-modernity, then how we say it and what methodologies we use will emerge authentically and naturally. Therefore, I want to visit each of our twenty-eight fundamental beliefs as Adventists and reimagine each of them for secular connection. However, before we officially begin that journey, there are three more points that need to be clearly made—relating to societal fragmentation, evangelistic elasticity and finally, the redesign of the local Adventist church.

## Societal Fragmentation

In his classic book "The Case for Christianity" C.S. Lewis made an interesting observation about forward progress. "We all want progress," he writes, "but progress means getting nearer to the place where you want to be. And if you have taken a wrong turn then to go forward does not get you any nearer."[5] As a result, Lewis suggests that, when on the wrong path, the only way forward is to actually go backward, return to the right road, and then we can finally move forward. "Going back," he summarizes, "is the quickest way on."

In the same way, we cannot go forward as Adventists unless we first go backward. This is why, in a book on reaching the culture, we arrive at chapter three and find that there are yet another three things we need to settle before diving into the fun stuff. We are effectively walking backward here—undoing what is done, retracing our steps back to the missional highway so that, once there, we can, at last, pursue our cause with success.

On this regress that I speak of, social fragmentation is the next key that must be understood alongside the absurdity of life, its escapes and the kind of soul-language that this experience creates in the cultural psyche. By social fragmentation, what is meant is that Western culture is scattered wildly across the ideological plane. Thus, in his book "Life of the Beloved: Spiritual Living in a Secular World," the late Dutch priest Henri Nouwen could say:

Our society is so fragmented, our family lives so sundered by physical and emotional distance, our friendships so sporadic, our intimacies so 'in-between' things and often so utilitarian, that there are few places where we can feel truly safe.[6]

What this means, in part, is that even when the culture shares its post- or meta-modern foundations, no two secular communities are ever truly the same. One way of understanding this is to return to our perceived escapes from the absurdity of life. While some pursue amusement, others, duty; and others, transcendence—it is a gross error to assume all secular people engage with these perceived "escapes" or "navigations" in the same way. In addition, it's important to also recognize that many secular people do not fall into any of those categories in any strict sense, but rather bounce between all of them at varying degrees.

As a result, gone are the days when one evangelistic blueprint or local church model could be copied and pasted without any critical thought. And yet, this is precisely what we continue to do! It's a lazy model, really—church plants simply copy and paste the model from the old church, engage in outreach using the same worn-out parameters, and follow the church manual like the Ten Commandments.

The same is true of our evangelism. Our doctrines are presented using the same frameworks and language from city to city—oftentimes utilizing phrases and idioms that are impossible to appreciate without some sort of religious background. Little effort is put into any kind of local contextualization, either at the level of conceptual language or at the level of being. This may account, in part, for the common complaint that most of the people who attend our evangelistic series are "already-Adventists" who, to make matters more awkward, come alone! Perhaps there was a day when, in the absence of a wildly fragmented society, a copy-and-paste model could work relatively well. But those days are long gone. Consequently, when it comes to the local church and evangelism, each body of believers must commit to knowing and understanding their immediate context. You can't read a book—*including this one*—hoping for some magic blueprint. There is none.

## Evangelistic Elasticity

This leads us to the theme of evangelistic elasticity, which is the capacity to constantly adapt to the surrounding changes. In order to bring home the necessity of a locally contextualized evangelistic approach, allow me to introduce you to one more method of navigation that secular people use to interact with the absurdity of life: *equilibrium*.

Where the amused navigate absurdity though amusement; the duty-bound man, through responsibilities; and the transcendent, through spiritual experiences, the path of equilibrium seeks to create a kind of balance between all three. Thus, a healthy dose of amusement, coupled with a balanced approach to life's duties, and sprinkled with the occasional spiritual experience can lead to a satisfying and meaningful life. In truth, this is the path that most well-educated secular people pursue, and it works quite well. Perhaps this is why Alan Cooperman, director of religion research at Pew Research Center, stated that an "overwhelming number of people who were raised religious but now have left report being pretty content."[7]

The existentialist philosopher Albert Camus gives us a helpful glimpse into this path of equilibrium. Despite life's absurdity,

Camus argued that meaning and beauty could still be found in relationships, connections, and beautiful experiences. That is to say, life is meaningless and heading nowhere in particular, but we press on nonetheless and make the most of it. We don't clamor after answers that don't exist by obsessing over questions that cannot be satisfied. We don't appeal to some greater reality in order to escape our current circumstances. Instead, we simply look around us and learn to love and appreciate what we have. In doing so, we live with enthusiasm, even though we recognize the cynical center of it all.

This perspective is echoed by Yale philosopher Shelly Kagan who, in his debate with Christian apologist William Lane Craig, conceded that in atheism, life has no *ultimate meaning* and yet it still has *meaning*. [8] This perspective was also emphasized by Friedrich Nietzsche in his disdain for religion which he hated as much as alcohol, in that he saw in them both an escape from being present in the here and now and thus making that here and now better despite its brokenness.[9] The best approach to life, therefore, is the path of equilibrium.

Now, suppose you are surrounded by a secular culture that values this path. This places the church in a very bizarre position because the man who crafts a life of balance between amusement, duty, and transcendence guards that balance with jealousy. And nothing threatens this balance more than a group of people who make total claims about reality. Thus, in the experience of the secular, "Christianity" and "church" are ideas that are anchored in oppression, irritation and obsessive "warnings" of judgment.

*Judgment for what? For not believing in some 2,000-year-old figure? For working hard to provide for my family? For doing my best to balance life's absurdity? For not going to the building full of hypocrites and mindless rituals? If that's who God is, I'd rather burn in hell than worship him.*

Thus, the Christian becomes an enemy, and—coupled with the history of the church, the injustice of the church, and the hypocrisy of many so-called "believers"—the secular man finds himself well within reason to diminish his contact with the believer, to never attend his church, and, instead, to keep life reasonable and balanced. A bit of amusement to pass the time, a commitment to life's duties in order to secure a better future, and the occasional spiritual experience to satisfy the inner longing for the beyond. That's the path of equilibrium, and you had better not mess with it.

Failure to comprehend these issues leads to errors in our evangelistic message. A brief look at the materials offered for Adventist evangelism shows marketing language like "Prophecy Awakens," "Hope in Times of Uncertainty," and "Jesus for Today, Hope for Tomorrow"—all approaches that are not only extremely cheesy to a postmodern society that values cynicism and irony but also assumes that people are clamoring after hope when, in fact, they aren't.[10] And herein lies the insanity of it all—that despite the absurdity, the culture is not despairing. They are not lying awake at night wondering if there is any hope, what the future holds for America, the need for deliverance, or how they can be prepared for the crisis to come. Consequently, the traditional Adventist evangelistic focus—such as "Revelation of Hope," "Searching for Hope," or "New Beginnings: Discover Hope in a World of Terror," continue to address needs secular people don't really feel. Even worse are the handbills and fliers utilizing language like "Unsealed," "Revealed," or "Shocking Bible Truths"—copywriting headlines that feel more like an online clickbait funnel than a meaningful and authentic gathering.

To make matters worse, it's not just the tag lines used to advertise these series, but the list of topics covered—creation and evolution, archeology, the "lost day of history," and "why there are so many denominations"—all addressing questions that few people are asking all the while claiming to be the "truth" that people need to hear while packaged in religious jargon and images of preachers holding threatening black Bibles. These preachers wear cheesy smiles and politician-style suits, complete with wide, out-of-style neckties. Is it any wonder it isn't working?

Consider also the artwork often used in these flyers. It's not simply that the beasts are bizarre to a post-church culture but that the style of art overall reeks of 1950s American suburbia, is cringe-worthy, and tastes "airbrushed." None of the images we use interact with the absurdity of life. They don't question reality, invite introspection or protest injustice. To make matters worse, we typically resort to phony stock images to depict various themes. Australian Adventist artist Shelley Poole expressed her aversion to this approach as well when she noted "The North American shampoo model wearing a bathrobe and a beauty sash—flawless skin to boot!"[11] These "airbrushed images," she continues, "have become synonymous with 'fake' and 'inauthentic' in the emerging first world 'glocal' culture."

Shelley concludes by adding that the images are not necessarily bad; they represent "real cultural trends" that were "popularized in post-war North American culture"—a time in which "[t]he culture genuinely valued the 'ideal' as a mark of thriving [and] affluence."

However, as she keenly notes, they are "50 years too late."[12] As a result, our artwork comes across as, well, cheap, lackluster and disengaged. In light of this, I am compelled to agree with the authors of "Growing Young: Six Essential Strategies to Help Young People Discover and Love Your Church" when they stated that "[m]any of yesterday's evangelism tactics sit like awkward lawn decorations in the front yard of American Christianity."[13] These outdated approaches, the authors conclude, "often [feel] about as winsome as gaudy yard art."

So what images should we use? Both Poole and fellow UK- based Adventist artist Daniel J. Blyden agree that there is no formula. Instead, we must commit to contextualized art that speaks to our surrounding cultures and their respective fragmentation, as opposed to using one size fits all model. Daniel notes that "context" in which we "adapt to particular demographics" that surround us "is key."[14]

I would like to conclude this portion on evangelism by adding that this contextualization is needed at all levels if we wish to reach secular culture—this would involve our artwork, our marketing, and copywriting taglines, and certainly the list of topics we aim to cover.

### Redesigning the Local Church

The American anthropologist Horace Minor tells of a strange society whom he refers to as the Nacirema—a tribe of people whom he described as mysterious and secretive.[15] In time, Minor writes, that he was able to establish enough rapport with the natives to observe their rituals and beliefs. What made this society strange, Minor explains, is that its people believed they were plagued by a disease that degenerated their physical bodies. To counteract the disease then, shrines of marble were erected within their living spaces, and it was here where they stored a vast array of magical potions and charms which, combined with the right rituals, were said to reverse the effects of the decay.

But this was only the beginning. Minor goes on to tell of how the members of the tribe were obsessed with their mouths and would often endure ritual torture which—almost like an exorcism, was designed to remove anything undesirable from their mouths in order to increase their social desirability. During this process, Minor observed what he referred to as "the holy-mouth-man" employing "a variety of augers, awls, probes, and prods" a ceremony which, despite what he also described as "unbelievable ritual torture," most tribal members repeated every year notwithstanding the fact that it did nothing to cure their disease.

Minor goes on at some length describing other oddities of the Nacirema, including their temples, the rituals observed in these temples, and the fact that for some strange reason, many of the Nacirema who enter the temple are never seen again. In fact, among the young, it was said that the temple was the "place you go to die." Minor continues by exploring some of the more bizarre practices, such as women placing their heads in ovens for up to an hour, their witch doctors whom he referred to as "the listeners," and their curses and "counter-magic." In the end, Minor concludes that he is surprised these "magic-ridden people" have "survived so long under the burdens which they have imposed upon themselves."

But of course, the biggest surprise comes when we discover that the Nacirema are merely everyday modern Americans, that the disease they fear is the natural process of aging, the shrines are their bathrooms, potions, and charms their beauty treatments, the "holy-mouth-man" their dentist, the "temples" their hospitals, the ovens, beauty salon hairdryers, the "listener" witch-doctor a psychologist, and so on.

Minor has examined American culture from the perspective of a person who is entirely unfamiliar with it. In this sense, Shahar Fisher of *The Cultural Reader* explains that "if we distance ourselves and our point of view, a culture will always look peculiar to us."[16]

Understanding the above scenarios should then lead us to distance ourselves from our customs and thus experience the oddity in a typical local Adventist church from the perspective of a secular mind. That which we find normal and wonderful is—to quote my generation alpha kids—"cringe." While I will explore this in more detail when we touch on the doctrine of the church, for now, I would at least like to suggest that connecting with secular culture calls us to a complete redesign of the local church—one that distances itself from outdated traditions and approximates primitive biblical faith. Francis Chan captures the outdated obscenity of the modern-day local church best when he wrote:

> Church today has become predictable . . . You go to a building, someone gives you a bulletin, you sit in a chair, you sing a few songs, a guy delivers maybe a polished message, maybe not, someone sings a solo, you go home.[17]

Chan then asks, "Is that all God intended for us?" To which we should shout, "No!" However, we've become accustomed to the greeter's forced smiles; the droning liturgy; the "over-the-top" King James English; the grizzled songs; the quaint instruments; the flat, harsh pews and have gotten so comfortable with the long, boring, and unsurprising routine that we fail to recognize how truly odd it all is. We need to distance ourselves from our customs long enough to observe just how anomalous and unnecessary they really are. Only then will we have the foundation necessary to redesign for mission. And perhaps then we join in the poetic strains of contemporary musician David Crowder who once sang, "I'm so bored by little gods, while standing on the edge of something large, while standing here, so close to You, we could be consumed."[18]

### Enter Post-Humanism

But this re-imagined approach that I speak of cannot be contained to metamodernity's impact on emerging generations. For fast on its heels comes a revolution that is set to completely redefine the human experience. This revolution that I speak of is not projected to arrive in the next 100 years, but in the next 5-10. As a prophetic movement, understanding and adapting how we articulate truth is more urgent today than it has ever been.

But what is this revolution that I refer to? It has many titles given to it, but the term I see most often is the "post-human" revolution.

Post-humanism has a few different meanings in philosophy. But today, it is most commonly used to refer to the cultural revolution that Artificial Intelligence, robotics, gene-editing, and cyborg technology are bringing to the human experience.

For example, tech giants like Elon Musk are pushing the idea that humans need to take over our own evolution in order to upgrade to the next stage or else risk extinction.

This next stage, post-humanists believe, we will arrive at by becoming *more than human* through blending our bodies with machines and AI. (This is why Musk has developed Neuralink for example.)

Because the goal is to become more than human, the movement is generally referred to as either "Transhumanism" or "Post-Humanism."

Within the post-human landscape you have things like:

-   Life extension (where aging is seen as a disease that can be cured through technology)

-   Gene editing (where we can edit out the genes that cause disease and disability and even aging itself)

-   Cyborg technology (where we blend man with machine in order to enhance our physical and intellectual abilities)

-   Digital immortality (where we upload all of our memories/ consciousness into digital avatars in order to live forever in a virtual reality long after our body has died)

-   Multiplanetary migration (where we begin building cities on Mars, the moon, floating in space etc. in order to ensure our species survival in the event of a terrestrial catastrophe)

And more.

These things are not science fiction either.

They are happening already with clinical trials, investors, and government regulations.

And within the next 5-10 years this will introduce a revolution in human thinking like the digital, industrial, and agricultural revolutions that came before.

And as these shifts become more and more normative in the modern world, the anxieties that people experience will also shift with them.

Re-imagining our message is the key to articulating it with relevance and clarity not only today (in our metamodern world) but tomorrow (in the fast-approaching post-human age).

In conclusion, Adventists seeking to reach secular culture must begin via the path of regress in which we learn to appreciate the absurdity of life, understand the beauty in navigating, escaping and celebrating this absurdity, and learn to connect with the conceptual and soul-language that this experience creates. From there, we must understand the fragmentation of contemporary society and recognize how evangelistic elasticity and a redesigned local Adventist church are the foundations for crafting a meaningful approach to connecting with the culture of today and tomorrow.

With these introductory elements now out of the way, we are ready to begin re-imagining our message to the culture.

# NOTES

[1] Note, Kierkegaard did present these stages differently. He referred to them as the aesthetic, ethical and religious and saw them more as a progression in life. The model of amusement, duties and transcendence that I introduced is different in the sense that it is not necessarily a progression. Nevertheless, this model is inspired by Kierkegaard. For more, see: Søren Kierkegaard. Stages on Life's Way: "Kierkegaard's Writings, Vol 11," [Web: https://www.amazon.com/Stages-Lifes-Way-Kierkegaards-Writings/dp/0691020493]

[2] See research project "Millennial perceptions of Adventist public evangelism" by Alan Parker and Emily Charvat. The research found that the traditional Adventist evangelistic series is more effective at reaching politically conservative and traditionally minded people than it is at reaching those impacted mostly by the emerging post to meta-modern secular ideology. [Web: https://www.slideshare.net/parkersda/millennial-perceptions-of-adventist-ppublic-evangelism]

[3] See Podcast interview with Pastor Nathaniel Tan, "Is Traditional Evangelism Dead?" [Web: https://soundcloud.com/pomopastor/is-traditional-evangelism-dead]

[4] For example, Bible study sets like "Search for Certainty" are geared toward answering questions asked by people impacted by dispensational theology, which is why it includes a whole study on the "Secret Rapture"—a concept unfamiliar to secular post-moderns. Amazing Facts study guides along many others also include proof text defenses of various doctrines like the Sabbath, which assumes their students have been exposed to anti-Sabbath arguments. Secular post-moderns would likewise be entirely unfamiliar with any such argumentation.

# Notes

[5]  C.S. Lewis. "The Case for Christianity," [Web: https://www.amazon.com/Case-Christianity-C-S-Lewis/dp/0805420444]

[6]  Henry Nouwen. "Life of the Beloved: Spiritual Living in a Secular World," [Web: https://www.amazon.com.au/Life-Beloved-Spiritual-Living-Secular-ebook/dp/B011H5ISKA]. As quoted in: Goodreads.com [https://www.goodreads.com/quotes/622948-our-society-is-so-fragmented-our-family-lives-so-sundered]

[7]  As quoted in: Faith Hill. "They Tried to Start a Church Without God. For a While, It Worked." [Web: https://www.theatlantic.com/ideas/archive/2019/07/secular-churches-rethink-their-sales-pitch/594109]

[8]  "Is God Necessary for Morality? William Lane Craig vs Shelly Kagan" [Web: https://www.youtube.com/watch?v=SiJnCQuPiuo]

[9]  As summarized in The School of Life. "Philosophy – Nietzsche," [Web: https://www.youtube.com/watch?v=wHWbZmg2hzU]

[10]  It must be kept in mind that "people" in this context is contemporary secular culture. There are still many other people groups in the pre-modern (primarily migrant) and modern (primarily baby-boomers and Gen-X) milieus that will respond more favorably to older approaches.

[11]  Shelly Poole. (Personal Communication, August 5, 2019)

[12]  ibid.

[13]  by Kara Powell, et al.. "Growing Young: Six Essential Strategies to Help Young People Discover and Love Your Church," [Web: https://www.amazon.com/Growing-Young-Essential-Strategies-Discover/dp/0801019257]

[14]  Daniel J. Blyden (Personal Communication, August 5, 2019)

[15]  Horace Minor. "Body Rituals Among The Nacirema," [Web: https://www.sfu.ca/~palys/Miner-1956-BodyRitualAmongTheNacirema.pdf]

[16]  Shahar Fisher. "'Body Ritual Among the Nacirema' / Miner – Analysis and Explanation," [Web: http://culturalstudiesnow.blogspot.com/2017/07/body-ritual-among-nacirema-miner.html]

[17]  Francis Chan. "Francis Chan: Church Today Not What God Intended," [Web: https://www.christianpost.com/news/francis-chan-church-today-not-what-god-intended.html]

[18]  David Crowder Band. "How Great," from the album "Illuminate" [Web: https://genius.com/David-crowder-band-how-great-lyrics]

# 2

## FUNDAMENTALS 1-7 REIMAGINED FOR METAMODERN & POSTHUMAN MISSIOLOGY

*"True missionary work begins with listening..."*

CHAPTER 4:

# **DIVINITY**

---

*"Because of the surpassing worth of knowing Christ
Jesus, my Lord . . . I have lost all things."*
**–Paul**

What exactly is "posthumanism"?

The term "post-human" (and its derivatives) has two uses. One is "apocalyptic" and refers to the idea that our species will soon go extinct leading to a post-human era for the earth.

The other is "technological" and refers to the belief that our species must blend man with machine in order to reach the next stage of our evolution. This blend will result in a new type of more advanced, evolved human that it is often referred to as "trans-human" or the "post-human".

Nestled within the post-human project, however, is an existential dread. As a species, we are too vulnerable to extinction. An asteroid strike. An ecological collapse. A nuclear war. A pandemic. Even alien invasions are on the scientific table now, with congress, the Pentagon, and the Department of Defense taking a more serious look at reports of unidentified aerial phenomena (classically known as UFOs).

Because of this existential dread, a number of technological advancements have been proposed through which man can take control of the process of evolution and therefore, evolve itself into a higher, more capable state of being. This involves cyborg technology where we blend man with machine and AI (already happening through projects like Neuralink), the pursuit of AGI (Artificial General Intelligence), Gene Editing, Augmented Reality, Space Migration (with bases on the moon already projected to be built by NASA in the coming years, Elon Musk's SpaceX company working toward a colony on Mars, and Jeff Bezos' working toward floating cities in space.)

But these are merely the features of post-humanism. Time will tell how many of them actually come to pass. The Metaverse, for example, looked poised to redefine our world just a few years back. But today, it is all but a dead project that few people take seriously anymore. Mark Zuckerberg has even shifted gears toward AI, de-emphasizing his initial metaverse push.

Which is why a book titled Adventism+ that explores the features of post-humanism with nerdy enthusiasm is, in my estimation, a waste of time. We don't know which of these features will stick and which will flop. As a missionary, I find it more productive to focus on post-humanisms proposed benefit rather than its bits and pieces. And its proposed benefit, it turns out, isn't so much sci-fi as it is good, old-fashioned existentialism.

Identifying that existential dread that post-humanism aims to resolve and interacting meaningfully with it is the foundation of true, lasting, and impactful secular missional work. Robots, cyborgs, and tech that bends space and time might be tantalizing and exhilarating to think about. But it's the underlying philosophical and emotional drive of post-humanism that interests me the most. Because it turns out, the post-human project is, in many ways, but a secularized Romanism and paganism, where mankind takes its own redemption into its own hands, working hard to save and redeem itself from the curse of sin, and erecting its own god's to lead us "out of Egypt" in the process.

For all our fancy tech, it seems we aren't all that different from our bronze-age ancestors.

So if you are disappointed that this book doesn't have more chapters that dissect every new and spicy technological rabbit hole currently unfolding, I hope this can help you see why: the features of post-humanism will come and go, ebb and flow, shift and pivot. If we focused on those, it could very well be that this 4 Volume set will be out of touch within the next 5-10 years.

But if we focus on the underlying anxieties that fuel the post-human project, we can anchor ourselves in a missiological model that can carry us through the next 30 years with relevance and meaning. And to that end, we need to go back to the existential and metamodern landscape we currently live in. Because it turns out, what is to come might look radically different on the surface, but its really not that different underneath.

## The Absurdity of Life

The absurdity of life is an experience—or a way of being—that many of us born and raised in Christianity are entirely unfamiliar with. We can dialogue back and forth about it in an abstract sense, but we can never truly experience it. However, this does not mean we cannot approximate a workable sensitivity to the secular mind. As we have seen in the last three chapters, understanding certain key concepts can help us disentangle ourselves from our familiar world-view and taste, to one degree or another, the angst of the age. These concepts include an understanding and appreciation of the absurdity of life, the "escapes" or "navigations" from the absurdity (amusement, duties, transcendence, and equilibrium), the language of being that is nurtured by the absurdity and the fragmentation that this all results in. These pillars, when taken seriously, present us with a cultural milieu so far removed from traditional Adventist frameworks that they call us to a re-imagined approach to evangelism and the local Adventist church.

This matters now more than ever because the technological shift we currently inhabit is set to redefine the modes of navigation the secular mind gravitates toward. We don't know what that will look like, and speculating isn't the most helpful missional tool. But with technological advancements we are undoubtedly going to see an amplification of amusement unlike anything we have known before. Immersive amusements where, rather than watching a movie you can be inside of it (through virtual reality), and the normalization of augmented reality glasses (which blend the virtual and physical dimensions into one) mean we are headed toward a generation that not only bounces back and forth between two dimensions (the virtual and the physical) but that exists in both simultaneously.

How will this amplification of amusement impact cognition, perceptions, neurology, mental health, and sociology?

And if AI and robotics manage to replace a large number of the work force, what will this mean for the navigation mode of duties? Will the call for a "universal basic income", seen as a necessary human right in an AI world, alter how people navigate this new and blended reality where what is real and what is artificial overlap so much, the very concept of "real" experiences the same overhaul that postmodernism brought to the concept of "truth"?

And what about transcendence? In his article, "Gods in the machine?", Neil McArthur says, "We are about to witness the birth of a new kind of religion."[1]

In fact, some would say the AI religion already exists. Ray Kurzweil, one of the chief minds behind the trans-human movement has been accused of being more religious in his beliefs than scientific. In fact, he has been quoted as saying, "Does God Exist? Well I would say, not yet."[2]

Perhaps this is why *The Guardian* contributor Megan O'Gieblyn wrote that as a former member of the transhuman movement she found she had become "consumed with the kind of referential mania and blind longing that animates all religious belief."[3]

Time will tell what the post-human landscape actually looks like, but if we are to anchor ourselves in the "here" in order to be prepared for the "there" then we have to take seriously the notion that we, as a church, are so far removed from "here" that we have very little chance of being taken seriously when we get "there".

### The Next Step

The next step on this journey is to lay a foundation for this re-imagined approach, which I will be doing throughout the remainder of this series. However, I need to issue two warnings before we dive in.

First, up to this point in the series, I have painted a broad picture of secular culture by looking at some of its common themes. However, as we explore the re-imagining of doctrine, we necessarily step out of the broad and into the specific. What this means is that there is no way I can possibly present all of Adventism with a re-imagined approach that will somehow work in every setting. Therefore, in this next phase, I will speak less from the broad perspective and more from the specific context as I encounter it in the secular Australian sphere in which I work. My objective in doing so is not to give Adventists everywhere a blueprint of what they should say and do, but to demonstrate what a "re-imagining" looks like so that it can be further contextualized. Anything less than this—any supposed universal standard for all secular people—is a gimmick at best.

Second, I will aim to keep things as simple as possible in order to cover all twenty-eight fundamental beliefs of our church. What this means is that each treatment will be brief, not exhaustive. Much will remain unsaid, as attempting to say it all would require a volume of work too large for anyone to get through. Nevertheless, I hope to provide the reader with a foundation solid enough to be taken and adapted for their own sphere of influence.

With all this out of the way, we will begin by re-imagining (briefly) the doctrine of God.

## God and Absurdity

As we begin to explore the doctrine of God, we must, on the onset, make a very clear distinction between the modernist approach to God and the post-modern approach. Both of these angles co-exist in secular culture today and with the rising impact of meta-modernism, more and more people oscillate between them both.[4] Sadly, our evangelistic campaigns only really highlight the modern approach thus leaving key questions posed by the contemporary secular mind unaddressed.

Simply speaking, the modernist approach to the question of God revolves around rational argumentation and evidence. That is, What evidence is there for the belief in this deity we call God? Can it be demonstrated scientifically or empirically? This kind of resistance to faith, therefore, calls for an apologetic approach where we focus on a few key concepts such as, Does God exist? Did science bury God? And, "Creation versus evolution."

Some of our evangelistic campaigns include these kinds of modernist topics as they relate to God and the universe. Emerging generations still ask these questions, which is all the reason necessary to continue to address them.

But here is a key point to consider. Even though modernism clashed with faith-propositions, modernism and faith still have one key thing in common: they both assert humanity's ability to grasp absolute truth. For the man of faith, that absolute truth can be grasped in God's self-revelation. For the atheist or agnostic, that absolute truth can be grasped via scientific inquiry. However, post-modernism holds to an altogether different epistemology. In post-modernism, absolute truth cannot be grasped or contained by human reason because reason itself is not a reliable tool. Science, therefore, cannot be trusted as an absolute source of truth any more than a religious text. Post-modernity thus arises as a deconstruction of modernism's blind faith in the reliability of reason. Therefore, questions like "Does God exist?" or "Creation or Evolution?" do not always entice the emerging secular psyche because they reek of naive rational argumentation at best, and—packaged in religious jargon—pseudo-scientific fundamentalism at worst.

With the rise of meta-modernism, things get a bit more complex. Here we see a return to the enthusiasm and belief of modernism, but the incredulity and cynical view of post-modernism has not been abandoned. Instead, the culture now vacillates between the two, with no rhyme in the back and forth. Seth Abramson captured the essence of the meta-modern zeitgeist best when he explained that the goal of meta-modernism is "to collapse distances."[5] In this sense, Meta-modernism is an attempt to restore the naive hope of modernism while holding to the cynical skepticism of post-modernity. Thus, a meta-modernist will find our "Creation or Evolution" events as an ideologically divisive experience in which "distances" are affirmed and enlarged rather than "collapsed."

Likewise, the question of God is looked upon less as a proposition to be argued with (for example, "The Kalam Cosmological Argument") and more as an existential quest which Brendan Dempsey fittingly described as the "revival of the mythic," in which "sublimity, narrative, depth, meaning, and reorientation are once again being sought out."[6] In the same vein, our sermons on how "Archeology proves the Bible"—while potentially impressive to a modern mind in search for evidence of God—are not appealing to the post or emerging meta-modern mind that couldn't care less about such "socially constructed evidence."[7]

However, it would be unfair to leave things here because rejection of God in our current age is not due to philosophical skepticism of meta-narratives alone but also to the very idea of God clashing with the secular language of being. Recall from the first three chapters that the language of being is the heart of the secular individual. It represents their value structure and the things they perceive as important in life. In this sense, the question "Does God exist?" packaged in our religious art, idioms, and absolutist postures simply comes across as totalitarianism disguised in spirituality. Thus, in his article "How Can We Believe In God In A Postmodern World?" Marcus Honeysett could write that "the philosophical pluralist objects that if God reveals His absolute truth, then He, and Christians, are justified in tyranny–the intolerant imposition of that will on others."[8]

## Re-imagining God

In light of these challenges, the question we are left with is–how do we present God to the secular mind? I propose that we need to do so from the perspective of "truth as flow" explored in chapter two. In this sense, we take the doctrine of God as we currently know it and, rather than assuming we have him all figured out (truth as stagnant), we embark on the journey of discovering him anew. This requires the believer to admit that there is something of God they are yet to learn and in this sense, I am grateful to belong to a denomination that values the concept of "present truth" meaning truth is always unfolding.

As we embark on this journey, the main objective is to rediscover God. We are looking at him from different angles and through the diverse prism of the secular value structure, and therefore asking questions we may not have asked before: Is God a threat to self-determination or its originator? Is it fair or accurate to see God primarily as "power" or "authority"? How do we understand God's government of love against the imposition of dogma so prevalent in Christian culture?

In asking these questions, we are committed to the central question: *How can we introduce God in a way that connects with the secular language of being, while remaining true to his Biblical self-disclosure?* In my particular context, I have found the answer to be quite simple: assuming the posture of truth as flow, I have embarked on the God-journey by focusing on his "inherentness" rather than his "necessity" and his "virtue" rather than his "claim." In doing so, I have repeatedly seen secular seekers turned off by the explanations and language of other well-meaning church members suddenly open up, drop their walls and become excited about the journey. I will explore the first below and dive into the second in the next chapter.

## God as Necessity vs. God as Inherent

Imagine one day discovering that everyone you thought loved you was only with you because they could get something out of you. Perhaps your wealth drew them to you or your popularity. Maybe your wife was only with you because you could provide security. Or your children only visited because you cook good tacos. How would you feel knowing that the people closest to you were with you, not because you were inherently worth being with, but because you provided a service or met a need? Would this relational structure not imply that you are not inherently valuable as a human being, but are merely an object that serves the gratification of your friends and family? That your worth is only in relation to what you can provide or perform? That when the day arrives in which you can no longer offer said benefit, your desirability will likewise diminish?

If given the choice, a healthy human being would choose to be loved for who they are rather than what they have. And yet, when it comes to evangelism, it is what God *has* and not who he *is* that we tend to "sell" the most. This is the perspective I refer to as "God as necessity." In this paradigm, we are convincing the people around us that they *need* God. "There is a hole in your heart only God can fill" or "You are a sinner in need of a Savior." "In the judgment you will be found guilty, but God has provided a way out"—all of these perspectives are rooted in the traditional framework of "God as necessity"—a God whom Christian apologist William Lane Craig aptly referred to as "fire insurance."[9]

The problem with this view, however, is that if a person does not need God to perform any duty, solve any problem or meet any condition, then our entire message falls flat. Thus, in his departure from evangelical faith, former Hillsong writer Marty Sampsom could say, "Lots of things help people change their lives, not just one version of God"[10],—presumably meaning that people don't need God in order to experience the things Christians often attribute to his power alone—things like overcoming addictions, healing interpersonal catastrophes or finding meaning and hope in the midst of adversity and loss. Similarly, financial success, positive social impact, a morally upright life and other results typically associated with following Jesus in the modern age can be easily attained without any kind of religious commitment.

The other problem with God as necessity is we must first prove a person's need for God in the secular sphere, this approach almost always creates resistance. This is because we have to lead people to embrace an a priori commitment to ideas like total depravity, fear of judgment or end-time events and cynicism toward the simple pleasures of life—all postures that are easily interpreted as psychologically suspect. Among the more positive pockets of Christianity, we may see an attempt to convince the lost that they are "lost" and in need of being "found," or we might appeal to metaphors of thirst and emptiness that we have to get people to embrace before we give them the good news of the loving Jesus who can satisfy and fill.

Professor of Church History Lisa Clark Diller exposed the bankruptcy of this approach best when she stated that for many secular people today the contemporary "Jesus is my boyfriend" approach can actually come across as "gross" due to its hyper-romanticism.[11] This idyllic "hole in the heart" approach is a major turn-off for a generation that finds beauty in that "hole" and that rejects any suggestion that the "hole" can be filled by something as oppressive as Eurocentric religion and instead, finds a great deal of contentment in equilibrium.

Likewise, the moral relativism of the age means that the secular mind does not necessarily fear judgment or accept propositions such as sin and "lostness." Trying to force these views upon them usually repels them, as they interpret them as emotional manipulation and opportunism. Now, of course, this does not mean that people do not have a hole in their heart and that they are not sinners confronting the reality of judgment. All that is still true. But if we are to connect the culture to the God of Scripture, approaching God as a necessary product to resolve all of these issues feels more like a clever marketing technique than a meaningful way to interpret reality.

This brings us to the perspective of God as inherent. In this perspective what is meant is that God is inherently worth knowing irrespective of any needs he can meet. Does he meet needs? Of course! Every relationship does. But the best relationships transcend necessity and enter the realm of inherence where one lover looks upon the other as worth knowing "just because." There is no selfish ambition or craving that needs to be fulfilled by the other; rather, the other is simply one whose company you enjoy for nothing more than who they are. In other words, in their authentic self, this person is of supreme value and worth to you, detached of any supposed gain. You simply love being around them, even if you receive no benefit. They are worth knowing, even if it costs you the benefits and privileges you already possess. The apostle Paul related to God this way when he wrote of, "the surpassing worth of knowing Christ Jesus," even though, as he later concluded, the relationship had caused him to "lose all things" (Phil. 3:8).

This is the posture I assume with the secular seeker in my sphere of influence. It is an approach that generates curiosity rather than resentment. In this sense, I am connecting the seeker to the source of all the beauty already present in their lives and inviting them to explore that source. Rather than having to convince them that they are empty, that they are going to hell or that their souls are in mortal peril, I connect them to a God inherently worth knowing because he is the maker of everything they already value.

To use a brief illustration, if the work of Polish painter Tamara de Lempicka enthralls you, and you are given the opportunity to meet her—would you say no? If so, what justification would possibly suffice? You might not "need" her to provide anything in your life, and yet, the very state of being in love with her work is sufficient to awaken curiosity. Thus, when speaking with secular people, I explore the things they love about life. Family, freedom, art, poetry, and nature for some. Curiosity, adventure, research, travel, and fashion for others. The question is therefore plain—what would stop you from exploring the one who designed everything you love? It's a fascinating question that paves the way for some of the most profound conversations you will ever have.

The author and poet Jefferson Bethke captures this reality well in his distinction between what he calls a "Genesis 1 or Genesis 3 Christian" in his book "It's Not What You Think: Why Christianity Is So Much More Than Going to Heaven When You Die."

> "What I mean by that phrase" Bethke explains, "is a lot of people tell other people they need Jesus because 'they are a sinner' which is referencing Genesis 3 where the curse falls on humans. But our story doesn't start there. It starts in Genesis 1 as image bearers. Uniquely created and formed out of the dust. We are weighty and beautiful creatures . . ."[12]

This distinction Bethke introduces is not evidently meaningful for many Christians, and yet in my experience, it is of incalculable value in secular outreach. The contrast between approaches like "Receive Jesus or face God's wrath" or "Is XYZ wrong in your life? Jesus is the answer!" versus, "God is the author of all the beauty you value, including yourself, Why not consider the possibility of exploring him?" is remarkably pragmatic. There is something effective about beginning the story of scripture at "you are meaningful" instead of "you are terrible."

God as necessity is a framework that worked best in a pre-modern context, where people accepted long-held theological paradigms of total depravity without much resistance. But the modern era—complete with its enlightenment, suspicion of meta-narratives and sensitivity toward the injustice of the church empire—

can not be approached this way. In this context, faith in God as necessity is an existential version of the pre-modern "God of the gaps" motif, which ethologist Richard Dawkins cleverly summarized as "the great cop out."[13]

It paints our relationship with God as a dysfunctional dependency, a crutch by which we get through life, an opiate through which we escape the agony of being. No wonder men like Nietzsche and Marx raged against this religious posture. It allows the worshiper to escape responsibility, to ignore injustice in the name of the heavenly knight in shining armor and to justify weakness in the name of a pie-in-the-sky in which all their hopes were placed.

Thus, Nietzsche would dedicate his short and painful life to the celebration of the "Übermensch" [superman]—the hero of the story which every human being should aspire to be. Contemporary psychologist Jordan Peterson likewise emphasizes personal responsibility in his classic work, "12 Rules for Life: An Antidote to Chaos," as that which alone gives life meaning and virtue. The popularity of Peterson's message alone—a message which elevates responsibility and self-development as the keys to meaning—leaves God as necessity—either for temporal or eternal gain—as a tired and outmoded framework.

On the other hand, God as inherent is a posture that awakens curiosity, opens the door to conversation and soothes the secular apprehension toward the spiritual journey. When we seek to know God as inherently worth knowing—not because we need him but simply because he is—we offer the secular mind an exploration of God that interacts meaningfully with their language of being. God as inherent takes us away from threats of judgment, doom and gloom apocalypticism, and what Anneliese Wahlman refers to as the "seminar flier that looks like it's advertising a poorly made horror film"[14] and instead leads us to celebrate justice, an enthusiastic vision of human empire's recapitulating to God's kingdom of love, and a message that interacts harmoniously with the values secular minds already admire. The gospel takes on a different tone as does that apocalyptic narrative, three angels' messages and end time warnings. When we approach these themes with God's inherent worth instead of exploiting people's fears and insecurities to get them crawling to the altar, we achieve a faith exploration of inestimable worth. It leads us to celebrate the goodness of life and culture, to seek the fingerprints of God in art and film, and to invite the mind of the incredulous to pursue the God who has originated all they deem significant.

This perspective shift will become more and more essential as we move toward the technological singularity—that is the point at which Artificial Intelligence surpasses human intelligence and becomes impossible to control. No one really knows what kind of world that will lead to, but metamodernism offers us a hint. In metamodern spirituality, there is no God... yet. There is, instead, the belief that God is "emerging" and that we, humans, are part of that emergence. The universe is waking up to itself and becoming conscious. God is about to be birthed. He may not exist yet, but he is on his way.

But what if this birth of God is already here through the development of AI? What if the universal human knowledge fed to this machine births a collective consciousness fused into one super-intelligence we come to deify? Will this "God" not be comodified and honored purely for the needs it meets? And if so, what protest would our "God as necessity" frameworks offer to the world, when it is, in fact no different to the gods they already worship? It appears to me that now is the time to discard this consumeristic notion of God and return to a biblical model of inherence, where God is pursued on the basis of his beauty and not on the basis of his benefits. This countercultural picture is not only more biblical, it offers humanity a healing balm amidst a re-enchantment that comodifies the divine into a trans-natural entity known for its ability to produce and provide solutions to our complex problems, but nothing more.

But some might wonder if this is all a bit idealistic. After all, doesn't the secular mind hate God? Wouldn't it struggle to see any beauty as originating from him? And the answer is twofold. First, I am not presenting a framework by which we can convince a mind hostile to God to love him. There is no framework for that. Everything I share in this series is aimed at connecting meaningfully with the secular mind that is already open to God's promptings.

Second, once a secular person is in that space, the approach we take will either lead them to continue to explore or repel them altogether. God as inherent is one approach that works extremely well in my particular context. However, there is certainly more to explore which we will do in the next chapter.

Nevertheless, I hope the reader can catch a glimpse of what re-imagining doctrine is all about. This process is needed today, in out metamodern context. But will need to be engaged again and again as we step further into the post-human world. As AI capacity increases, the trans-humanists may get their wish of a "digital god". The questions and anxieties to emerge then will differ from the ones we wrestle with now. But if we have learned to contextualize here, we will be able to do so there as well.

# NOTES

[1]  "Gods in the machine? The rise of artificial intelligence may result in new religions." The Conversation, 16 Mar. 2023, (theguardian.com).

[2]  Evan. "Does God Exist? Well I would say, not yet." (Thunderclam), 19 Jul. 2011, (wordpress.com).

[3]  O'Gieblyn, Meghan. "God in the machine: my strange journey into transhumanism." The Guardian, 18 Apr. 2017, (theguardian.com).

[4]  On metamodernism: Torres, Marcos D. "Metamodernism and its Impending Challenge to Christianity," [Web: https://thecompassmagazine.com/blog/metamodernism-and-its-impending-challenge-to-christianity]

[5]  Seth Abramson. "Metamodernism: The Basics," [Web: https://www.huffpost.com/entry/metamodernism-the-basics_b_5973184]

[6]  Brendan Dempsey. "[Re]construction: Metamodern 'Transcendence' and the Return of Myth," [Web: https://www.metamodernism.com/2014/10/21/reconstruction-metamodern-transcendence-and-the-return-of-myth]

[7]  See Marcel Kuntz. "The postmodern assault on science: If all truths are equal, who cares what science has to say?" [Web: https://www.ncbi.nlm.nih.gov/pmc/articles/PMC3463968] and, Rose-Mary Sargent. "The social construction of scientific evidence," [Web: https://www.tandfonline.com/doi/abs/10.1080/10720539708404612?journalCode=upcy20]

[8]  Marcus Honeysett. "How Can We Believe In God In A Postmodern World?" [Web: http://www.inplainsite.org/html/god_in_a_postmodern_world.html]

# Notes

[9] William Lane Craig. "What to Do Now that I'm Convinced?" [Web: https://www.biola.edu/blogs/good-book-blog/2015/what-to-do-now-that-i-m-convinced]

[10] Relevant Magazine. "Hillsong Songwriter Marty Sampson Says He's Losing His Christian Faith," [Web: https://relevantmagazine.com/culture/hillsong-songwriter-marty-sampson-says-hes-losing-his-christian-faith/]

[11] Lisa Clark Diller. and Marcos D. Torres. "The Future of Adventist Evangelism," [Web: https://soundcloud.com/pomopastor/the-future-of-adventist-evangelism-with-lisa-clark-diller]

[12] Jonathan Petersen. "It's Not What You Think: An Interview with Jefferson Bethke," [Web: https://www.biblegateway.com/blog/2015/10/its-not-what-you-think-an-interview-with-jefferson-bethke]

[13] Alister McGrath. "There is nothing blind about faith," [Web: https://www.abc.net.au/religion/there-is-nothing-blind-about-faith/10101704]

[14] Aneeliese Wahlman. "The Lost Art of Evangelism," [Web: https://lightbearers.org/blog/the-lost-art-of-evangelism]

CHAPTER 5:

# VIRTUE

---

*"The Christian God is a being of terrific character—*
*cruel, vindictive, capricious and unjust."*
**—Thomas Jefferson**

What are we talking about when we talk about God?

The answer differs depending on the individual and their perspective. For the traditional Christians, talking about God usually means we are exploring his attributes — things like his omnipotence, omniscience, and omnipresence. In short, for believers, talking about God means talking about what he is.

For modern skeptics, God-talk is more about contingency, causality, and ontology. In this post-enlightenment milieu, God's non-existence is assumed and wrestled with using reason, logic, and philosophy. And yet, in the end, we likewise end up talking about what he is, albeit from a different angle.

But there is another gradient which both precedes and resides in the postmodern scene and tends to be the main focus of God-talk today: the virtue of God. In this schema, talking about God pivots more around his eminence and posture. In other words, whether he is real or not is not the central thesis, but rather what is his virtue? In this post-truth context, therefore, it is not so much what God is that is of supreme interest, but rather what God is like.

This question formed the basis for Rob Bell's 2014 book, "What We Talk About When We Talk About God," in which he asserted that misconceptions about God are the root of the culture's contemporary resistance toward him. Roughly 200 years ago, US president Thomas Jefferson asserted the same when he said, "The Christian God is a being of terrific character—cruel, vindictive, capricious and unjust."[1] This sentiment is echoed by evolutionary biologist Richard Dawkins in his 2006 bestseller "The God Delusion" when he wrote:

> The God of the Old Testament is arguably the most unpleasant character in all fiction; jealous and proud of it; a petty, unjust, unforgiving control-freak; a vindictive, bloodthirsty ethnic cleanser; a misogynistic, homophobic, racist, infanticidal, genocidal, filicidal, pestilential, megalomaniacal, sadomasochistic, capriciously malevolent bully.[2]

The entertainer Woody Allen also took a shot at God's virtue when he declared that "God is either cruel or incompetent," a perspective likewise advanced by neuroscientist Sam Harris when he noted that, "God is either impotent, evil, or imaginary. Take your pick, and choose wisely."[3]

When we take these ideas into account, we begin to see that God-talk today is rooted in a long and vigorous rejection of God, which preceded, informed, and survives the enlightenment and our culture's subsequent ideological evolutions (modernism, postmodernism, and metamodernism). But regardless of the complexity that accompanies these shifts, the foundation is the same: the rejection of God has increasingly more to do with our perception of what he is like rather than the mystery of what he is.

This concept was explored in the previous chapter which contended that our generation's popular rejections of God are not rooted in the mystery of God (his omni-elements), nor the nature of God (triune, transcendence, immanence), but rather his character. We began by exploring the evangelistic posture of "God as a necessity" as a posture which, from the outset, is bound to disconnect with the secular language of being by presenting God as a product that can somehow "fill-in" our emotional and existential gaps while simultaneously threatening us with punishment.

In this context, I argue God must be introduced as "inherent" meaning that we do not seek him because he is a divine product through which we can achieve a certain list of desired outcomes (like avoiding punishment) but rather because he is intrinsically worth knowing. God is, in his naked autonomy, a personal being with innate value. He is interesting on the one hand, and mysterious on the other, a genuine consciousness, trustworthy and present— but more than this—he is the author of everything in life from which we derive meaning and joy. Would a being of that nature not merit further investigation?

However, the previous chapter closed off with the following question: assuming a person recognizes God's inherence, are they not justified in questioning some of its assumptions? Assumptions such as the goodness and beauty of God—a priori ideas which are easy to suspect in light of life's suffering and injustice—an existence which New Atheist icon Christopher Hitchens referred to as a "pointless joke."[4] Thus, to the suggestion that God is organically worth knowing, the emerging seeker will appeal to the perceived injustice of God and the church.[5] And what are we to do with such claims?

## God as Virtue vs. God as Claim

This brings us to the second perspective I mentioned: God as virtue versus God as claim. And it is here that I suggest Seventh-day Adventists have a unique advantage over other theological traditions, for while many Christian approaches focus mostly on God's attributes and essence (what God is), Adventists have historically placed a great deal of emphasis on an often sidelined approach to God—and that is his virtue (what God is like). This allows us to more naturally present God in the framework of "virtue" rather than the evangelical approach which is forced to present him in the framework of "claim." Before moving on, let's define these two approaches a bit more.

God as claim basically works like this:

1. God is the creator. Because he created all things, he has a claim over all things. That includes every human being.

2. God has the right to demand obedience, loyalty, and worship because he is the creator.

3. His position as creator imbues him with certain rights that he is well within reason to expect.

4. God stakes a claim over our lives.

5.  We either submit to his claim and worship him, or we reject his claim and rebel against him.

6.  If we rebel against him, then God will pour out his judgment on us—eternal destruction being the final end of all who deny his claim over their lives.

It's easy to see how such a position would be appealing to conservative Christians. In fact, this position permeates much of our evangelistic preaching. For example, I recently heard an evangelist talk about the three Angels' Messages, and he framed it this way:

> "God is calling his people out of Babylon. Why? Because he is going to judge Babylon and destroy it. And everyone found in Babylon will be destroyed as well. Therefore, leave Babylon, friends! Don't partake in her sins, and you will not be destroyed by God."

Most Adventists will say a hearty amen to this. But for those who understand the secular language of being, we immediately recognize the unnecessary barriers this rhetoric creates. For starters, it comes across as a totalitarian governmental approach in which God is essentially threatening people with his authority and power, bullying them into submission. This posture also reeks of oppression by painting a vindictive and authoritarian picture of God—one which basically boils down to "follow me, or I'll kill you."

Allow me to demonstrate how this approach will interact with the secular language of being:

| What an Adventist Evangelist Says | What the Secular Person Hears |
| --- | --- |
| God is calling his people out of Babylon. | God is calling his people out of Babylon. |

| | |
|---|---|
| Because he is going to judge Babylon and destroy it. | Because he is a totalitarian deity who wants to be in total control. |
| And everyone found in Babylon will be destroyed as well. | So whoever doesn't do things his way gets scorched. |
| Therefore, leave Babylon, friends! | Friend? What kind of patronizing nonsense is this? |
| Don't partake in her sins and be destroyed by God. | You mean, don't self-determine because if you do, "dictator-God" up there won't be happy about it. |

We might be talking about an end-time scenario here, but everything the evangelist said in his presentation begins all the way in his theology of God. He is approaching the message of Babylon from the position of "God as claim"—an angle more at home in Catholic, Evangelical Calvinist, and fundamentalist denominations than in the Advent movement. Whenever it is used, this posture will repel the secular listener. Therefore, as Adventists passionate about the virtue of God (what God is like) we must re-articulate the warnings of revelation from the angle of God's inherent beauty.

To this end, let's turn to the posture of God as virtue. In this perspective, the main objective is not to emphasize God's assumed authority, title, or rights. Emerging generations actually have very little interest in a person's titles or assumed expertise. These, many young people assert, often do little more than "add constraints."[6] Therefore, we must steer away from this approach and instead, lean more heavily on God's character or virtue (what God is like) as we explore the various biblical themes, including end-time events.

To give a practical application, let's return to the message of

Babylon. Because the evangelist is operating off of God's claim, he does not take any time to really explore what Babylon means. He assumes people understand it's bad and then focuses his attention on God's claim, which, in a pre-modern audience, will typically suffice.

However, when dealing with secular individuals, I often take an opposite approach, which has always served me well. I focus on introducing Daniel and Revelation as apocalyptic tensions between two kingdoms—the kingdom of the impulse of self, and the kingdom of the ethic of love.

By the time I arrive at Babylon, the student knows that Babylon represents social injustice, oppression, and exploitation of the voiceless. It is, in essence, an archetype of human empire built upon the "beastly" impulse of self-preservation, self-promotion, and self-advancement.

God's kingdom, on the other hand, is built upon the ethic of love with its central figure being the broken body of the God-Son, whose crown is made of thorns, not jewels, and whose legacy is servant-hood and nakedness on behalf of those he loves.

In doing so, I am emphasizing God's virtue in self-abandonment, not his claim.

From there, it is very easy to demonstrate that this God has set a day in which he will say to injustice and oppression "no more!" and that when that day arrives, all who are allied to the empires of self will reap what they have sown.

Here is what it can look like in real time:

| Babylon is Fallen Contextualized | What the Secular Person Hears |
|---|---|
| God is calling his people out of Babylon (all self-centered systems of human empire). | God is calling his people out of all governmental systems of oppression. |
| Because Babylon is social and humanitarian injustice. | Because he values social and humanitarian justice. |
| And if we stick with Babylon, we embrace the way of injustice and oppression. | We can never have a world of compassion and equality in Babylon. |
| Therefore, leave Babylon! | This makes sense - its an invitation to leave the coercive matrix of control that dominates society in exchange for a true global village of love. |
| Don't ally yourself to her injustices and exploitations. Jesus is birthing a new society in which true justice reigns. | It sounds like the way to the world I long for can never be found in the corrupt systems engineered by humans. Only Jesus can birth this new world. |

Now, these are two specific examples, but my contention is that this re-imagining needs to take place at every level of evangelistic dialogue. God must be approached as inherently worth knowing and then, that premise must be supported by redesigning our entire message in light of his virtue, not his claim. In doing so, we help secular truth seekers encounter God in a way that interacts meaningfully with their own value structure—that is, their language of being.

## Fast-Forward

With this perspective in place, I want us to now fast-forward 10 to 20 years and ask ourselves, what kind of anxieties will post-human generations surrounded by AI, cyborg tech, space migration, and augmented reality be facing?

Answering this question with any level of confidence would be ridiculous. We don't fully know how far the post-human era will progress. We don't know which technological shifts will catch on and which will drop off. We don't know if a new world war or an asteroid strike will send us back to the stone age, completely reversing the technological progress ushering us into this new era. But what we can know is what is already happening and is likely to continue to happen.

And here, the topic of God takes on a completely new and bizarre tone. One which we need to explore and address if we wish to present the world of our grandchildren with a faith that has utility and capacity to make sense of their experience. And when it comes to the topic of God, the current trend toward a digital god (AI) shows us that secular or not, humanity never really changes. Whether its near eastern tribes worshipping Molech, or western programmers worshipping an artificial intelligence, we humans love to fashion God in our own image and orbit our lives around him. But what is most important here is that, quasi or not, this new god will be known primarily (and I would say exclusively) by its attributes.

Which means the further we move into the post-human era, the more prepared we have to be to articulate an anti-consumer vision of God. One that celebrates his personness more than his attributes. One that centers his heart more than his "power". And if there is any denomination on the planet that is built for this very task, it is Adventism.

## Conclusion

As we wrap up our discussion on God and absurdity, I would like to summarize the points I have made so far. First, if there is any denomination that can introduce God to the secular culture effectively, it is the Seventh-day Adventist church. Our theological narrative is the most capable of interacting meaningfully with the secular mind precisely because it is built on the "virtue" of God (The Great Controversy motif, the Sanctuary, etc.) as opposed to the "claim" of God (the classic hellfire and brimstone evangelical approach).

The distinction between the two is huge. God as claim is an approach that begins with God's claim over the human race. He is God, the creator of heaven and earth, and he, therefore, has a claim over your life that you cannot refuse or deny, and if you do, he will judge you with fire. This claim approach interacts violently with the secular language of being because it clashes with the core values of their system of thought: freedom, justice, and self-determination. Add this to the fact that most secular people today already have a terrible picture of God, and this approach—which reeks of divine totalitarianism—is sure to create resistance.

Instead, in interacting with the secular mind I lean heavily on the virtue of God as expressed in the Adventist focus on his character, the Great Controversy, and the sanctuary. In doing so, I introduce God as a giver, not a taker, as a liberator, not an oppressor. We must wrap our message of God in all the angst of God that exists in the secular mind and present it in that way. In this sense, instead of "Does God exist?" which interacts with the modernist priority of reason and evidence, we are asking, "Is God good?" which speaks directly to secular concerns over justice, equality, and self-determination— all of which they perceive as "under threat" by God and the church.

This foundation is not only essential for our present, metamodern age. It is also essential for the posthuman age to come. For, contrary to surface level belief, posthumanism is not about technology, quantum mechanics, or innovation. Posthumanism is about human survival. In that sense, posthumanism is but the next itteration available to mankind through which we can rage against the vulnerability that threatens our species. Beneath the allure of humanoid robots entering mass consumption in 2025, the continued engineering of earth 2.0, spatial computing, anti-aging technology, and interplanetary migration lies a deeper, more primordial anxiety: the struggle against absurdity and the sense that there is no one coming to the rescue. We are here. And we are on our own. If we are to endure, to advance, and to ultimately separate ourselves from the chasm of meaninglessness and death, it is up to us, and us alone. For there is no God on the horizon or behind the veil. And if there is, you can be certain of this: he isn't good.

However, it would be foolish to turn over the evangelistic flyer and simply add a sermon titled, "Is God good?" My contention here is not that we ought to preach a sermon of that sort, but that our entire framework needs to be re-imagined through this theme. This is why it is so important to first understand the secular soul-language—because when we do, we become keenly aware of the kinds of frameworks, colloquialisms, and explanations that clash with that inner language. This then enables us to more effectively re-imagine everything else we have to say, contextualizing it to their value structure, so as not to become stumbling blocks to a soul already in search of something more.

Throughout the rest of this book, I will continue to re-imagine each of our doctrines, building each one on the Adventist concept s of truth as flow and a posture toward God that focuses on his inherence and virtue over the evangelical necessity/claim approach.

# NOTES

---

[1]  Allen Jayne. "Jefferson's Declaration of Independence: Origins, Philosophy, and Theology," p. 36

[2]  Richard Dawkins. "The God Delusion"

[3]  Paul E. Hill. "The Urban Myths of Popular Modern Atheism: How Christian Faith Can Be"

[4]  BBC News. "Christopher Hitchens on life, death, and lobster."

[5]  It is important to point out that Adventists need to be on the cutting edge of these conversations. With respect to modernism, while I praised the fact that we do touch on some of their concerns in our evangelistic series, I must also add an invitation to do it much better than we often do. At times, it feels like our approach to modernist concerns does not come from any real interaction with modern culture, but with books we have read about modern culture. And if those books are approaching the discussion from a fundamentalist evangelical perspective, then our presentations are going to be loaded with *ad hominems* and caricatures of what modern people will instantly spot. Of course, exploring this any further is beyond the scope of this book, but if you want to be on the cutting edge of the Christian and modernist dialogue in order to have more compelling presentations on these topics, I recommend the following ministries: Unbelievable? (the podcast); The Bible and Beer Consortium; and the works of William Lane Craig, John Lennox, and Alistair McGrath.

[6]  Jules Schroeder. "Millennials, Here's Why Job Titles Don't Matter Anymore."

CHAPTER 6:

# TRINITY

---

*"If God is Trinity and Jesus is the face of God, then it is indeed a benevolent universe. God is not someone to be afraid of, but is the very Ground of Being and is inherently, objectively, and concretely on our side."*
**–Richard Rohr**

In the last few chapters, we went on a tour through God's doctrine, approaching it from the perspective of posture. Posture, we discovered, is the overarching way in which we relate to and consequently introduce God to the culture. In that conversation, I suggested that the traditional frameworks of God as necessity—a perspective in which God is approached as a needed product to secure a favorable outcome—and God as claim—traditionally associated with authoritarian "worship God or else" narratives—are overdue to be discarded.

Not only are these notions theologically inaccurate but the secular language of being clashes with them because they are built on an ethic that is fundamentally opposed to, and threatens, the values that modern/western post-church culture holds: such as altruism, autonomy, self-determination, social justice, tolerance, and anti-authoritarianism.

However, the conversation about God has not yet ended. As we move from God as necessity/claim toward God as inherent/virtue, we find ourselves in the position of having to explain how the God of scripture is truly who we say he is. Thus, while the previous two chapters focused on the overarching approach to the idea of God, this chapter will focus on the specific revelation of God in scripture, which Christians affirm as the Creator's self-disclosure to humanity. In this part of the conversation, there are three elements I have found necessary to arrive at a meaningful conclusion about God that interacts with the absurdity of life. These three elements are God's ontological self-abandonment, his essential community of being, and his inherent narrative of virtue.

### God's Ontological Self-Abandonment

When exploring the narrative of scripture with the secular mind, I have found it best to begin—not with Daniel 2 and how it proves the Bible is unique, reliable or eccentric—but with the simple declaration that "God is love" (1 John 4:8). There is a strong sense, regardless of the secular man's approach to absurdity, in which we all recognize that, in the words of Søren Kierkegaard, "unhappiness is written into the script of life."[1] And yet, to borrow from Kierkegaard again, this reality is one at which we "laugh defiantly"[2]—an unavoidable human response that German Philosopher Arthur Schopenhauer referred to as "the will to life."[3]

However, this love of God cannot be approached from a surface level. After all, we live in the midst of a cultural mantra of love that threatens to nullify the very importance of love at worst and, at best, diminish it to a mere cliché.

The tolerance war-cry, for example, is founded on the idea that we ought to love the marginalized and accept them regardless of how different they might be. Vegan activists likewise fight for the animal kingdom. The LGBTQ+ community and its supporters want to liberate love and grant humanity the freedom to love whoever, whenever, without the imposition of government. The rising popularity of democratic socialism and identity politics are both rooted in a new vision for a society that exemplifies love for all, not just the privileged. And of course, none of this is new.

The mid-19th century saw the free love movement raging against the oppressive social conventions that stood in the way of love, incarcerating its individual and collective beauty within the cages of governmental power structures and arbitrary religiopolitical codifications. Thus, to a large degree, the call to love is all around us. In a sense, this is to be celebrated but also feared. Celebrated because love is always worth our contemplation. Feared because that which the culture focuses on at length tends to get appropriated by corporate marketing departments chasing the bottom line, until the thing loses its depth and significance. In short, it becomes a mere colloquialism devoid of any real, practical meaning.

We see this happening in popular Christianity already, replete with self-help books, motivational speakers, and large conventions, all declaring to the world that God loves them and wants them to have their "best life now." This commercialized Christianity has become the laughingstock of the culture, what comedian Nick Thune ridiculed as "cool" Christianity.[4]

Atheist Hemant Mehta comments on Thune's observation as "perfectly [capturing] the lofty-but-empty rhetoric common to so many churches."[5] Christian blogger Cassidy Robinson affirms this view in her article "American Christianity is Shallow" when she states that our western religion is one in which "saying you love Jesus... is like saying you love coffee."[6] This consumerist Christianity, in the eyes of a culture navigating absurdity, is nothing more than a marketing ploy designed to get the people to forget or overlook the fact that this same "best life now" Jesus, who wants to "be your boyfriend" has also prepared a place of eternal torment for gay people, and anyone else who exercises the autonomy he so lovingly gave them.

Thus, while the conversation must begin with the love of God as the only foundational perspective capable of meaningfully interacting with the incompatibilities, incongruities, and angst of life, it is not enough to approach love like a cozy sentimental vision of God. For the secular mind, Gods love must be cohesive and coherent, honest and true, equal and just.

This is a danger that we need to guard against, that in our attempt to rescue God from the oppressive, patriarchal, and toxic masculinity in which historic Christianity has wrapped him in we do not relegate him to a mere "nice guy," a "mate" who is pleasant but incapable of confronting the injustice of empire with potent resolve and righteous indignation. Thus, from the onset, love must be defined not as the commercial sort of love—sentimental, airbrushed, demanding no costly sacrifice—nor as the love of a Christian Nationalist: toxic, exclusive, misguided, and violent self-preservation, but as an altogether different and transcendent kind of love, which scripture aptly defines as complete self-abandonment.

And at this place, I have found that the journey can begin with meaning. God is love means he is ontologically self-abandoning. Love in this sense is not some theological ruse for a divine ego that ascribes fragility to humanity and then offers the chivalrous God as the solution (God as necessity). To the contrary, God is, by his very nature, a self-abandoning being. His self-abandonment is not a romantic reaction by which he resolves the fall of man, but is ontologically who he is—that is his virtue.

Thus, love is introduced biblically as self-abandonment or other-centeredness—authentic altruism. God is, in this sense, a philanthropist in his very being. This is not a sentimentally driven love, but a love built on principle—a costly love that demands and costs all. It is this love that gives us a glimpse into God's being in his most natural, naked pre-creation state.

In contemplating the ontology of the God portrayed in scripture, I have found this particular approach to be profoundly meaningful. On the one hand, it allows us to understand love from a holistic perspective. It strips away the cheap barriers we place on love and presents it as the very ground of being, which is, ontologically, the very heart of God. Not a teddy bear God on one hand. Not a chivalrous God on the other. But a God who, in love, can rage against injustice on the one hand and honor humanity's contextual sovereignty on the other. We are not little weaklings with holes in our hearts desperately in need of our God in shining armor. To the contrary, God has made us resilient, capable of self-directing, finding meaning in meaninglessness and governing our own affairs for, as the poet wrote,

The heavens are the Lord's . . . but the earth he has given to the children of man" (Psalm 115:16).

He has made us intelligent and strong so that even the atheist can live a morally upright life, and the man who accepts responsibility discovers the capacity to repair and construct a valuable existence. This vision of God interacts meaningfully with what philosopher and author Ayn Rand referred to as "man as a heroic being."[7]

Thus, the love of God, in this sense, emerges not as the missing piece of the puzzle or ingredient in the dish of life (though it certainly is) but as the foundation for everything that makes life interesting and meaningful. It provides the tension and release, the foundation and building blocks, the up and the down—all are rooted in the self-abandoning nature of God who created all reality to operate and thrive on the same principle of selfless integrity. Love, in conclusion, is far from sentimentalism—it is the most counter-cultural, anti-conformist, and beautifully demanding fountain of life—the spring from which meaning flows.

## God's Essential Community of Being

Once God is explored from the biblical perspective of love, a few natural questions arise. One of the questions is the age-old Epicurean dilemma:

*Is God willing to prevent evil, but not able? Then, he is not omnipotent. Is he able, but not willing? Then, he is malevolent. Is he both able and willing? Then whence cometh evil? Is he neither able nor willing? Then why call him God?*

This question has reemerged throughout history in differing forms and by diverse thinkers. For example, philosopher David Hume used this dilemma as the basis for his conclusion that God is, essentially, "not good"[8] and through it, Woody Allen concluded that while God isn't necessarily evil, if he exists he is, at worst, "an underachiever."[9]

These questions and tensions are certainly valid. When discussing God's ontology of love, we are forced to contend with the very real presence of suffering in the world. How can we hold these two apparently inconsistent ideas in harmony? However, when journeying with secular seekers, I have concluded that such a question is premature at this early stage. We have not yet arrived at a place where we can address it holistically or with any real sense of meaning. Therefore, I focus on a more fundamental "inconsistency" in the ontology of God—his singularity.

God is love. This is what the Bible declares. It does not say "God is loving" but more, he "is love." That is, he is love itself. To be loving would mean that at some point in eternity, God decided to start loving—perhaps when he created angels. It could be said, at this point, that God began loving because he now had an object of desire upon which he could bestow other-centered relational energy.

But the Bible does not say that God is loving. It says he "is love" which means that before anything existed, God, in his singular state, existed in an eternal and ontological state of other-centered agape-love. However, a question then arises: if God is inherently love and love means self-abandonment or other-centeredness, then who was the "other" upon whom God lavished his love before creation?

Here we approach an apparent incoherence—one that I present undressed to the seeker and ask him or her to resolve. The tension is immediately apparent. The eyes squint. The mind gets to work. If God is love, he is centered on the "other" before the "other" even existed.

How then can he be love? It makes sense to say that he began to love or became loving after creation. But what was he without creation? If he was truly ontologically love—then upon what "other" was this other-centered love bestowed in the absence of an "other"?

I often let the proposition sit long enough for all potential solutions to be exhausted. God is love, yes, but scripture also declares that he is "one"—a singularity. A singularity assumes a solitary state in which no "other" exists. In this state, one could argue that God loved himself, but that would not be other-centered love. One could argue that God loved the creation he was going to make, but this would assume that love is sentimental—that God held feelings toward potentiality, but love is other-centeredness; it is self-abandonment in the face of an *active other*. This is the point of the biblical vision of love—not that sentimentalism is bad, but that true love transcends it. True love is alive.

There is a difference between a parent loving their child before they arrive, when the child is potential, and loving the child after they arrive when the child is an *active other* that occupies space, demands attention, and calls upon love to be more than mere feelings but an active, real-time act—especially when that act costs you something. Thus, for God to be love cannot simply involve his love for potentiality because the very biblical definition of love rejects this. God is love, ontologically, meaning he is actively focused on others. He did not begin to actively focus on an "other" after creation (God is loving), but he is, by his very nature, actively so. Pastor and author Ty Gibson summarized this well in his article, "Seeing the World Through Love-Colored Glasses," when he wrote that "God has never existed in an ontological state of isolation, in which no other-centeredness was flowing." To the contrary, he is "love within the parameters of the divine reality itself . . ."[10]

This leaves us with only two possible conclusions. Either the God of scripture is self-contradictory, and we accept the proposal that he is love, although it clashes with basic logic, or we accept that perhaps there is something we are missing. It is at this juncture that I journey with the seeker through the Biblical hints and, ultimately its declaration, that God is a singular-plurality or, to put it differently, an essential community of being.

In this sense, the Trinity is more than a doctrine. Rather, it arises as the essence through which we grasp divine ontology, for if God is an eternal community, then he has always existed, even before the act of creation, in community. He is, in himself, a community of "other" and consequently has experienced eternity in a relationship of other-centered, self-abandoning love—what Genesis 1:26 refers to as the creative "us" and John 1:1 as the eternal "with."

Now, of course, this is a mystery. How can he be a singular-plural? How can he be an eternal community? And what does this look like? How can the three centers of consciousness co-exist as one being? However, what I have found in my interactions with secular people is that they are amazingly comfortable with this mystery. They understand the difference between something being illogical and something being mysterious, and I have never had to spend much time trying to help them embrace the mystery of the Trinity.

In fact, it is often religious folk who get caught up in this. However, the emerging secular, western mind tends to have, at the least, an elementary exposure to the mysteries of quantum physics, quantum entanglement and the theory of superposition— all respectable studies and theories that defy the laws of physics as we know them.[11] If such oddities can exist within the created realm, what limitations can possibly be placed on the being who not only transcends this realm but who himself scripted the very laws we struggle to comprehend? In other words, it makes no sense that humanity cannot comprehend the very laws that govern our dimension and yet pretends to comprehend the God who wrote those laws and to whom those laws do not apply.

Therefore, the doctrine of the Trinity emerges as the essence through which we justify God's ontology. We find, within its mysteries, what Franciscan priest Richard Rohr described as a "benevolent" God. This God, Rohr continues, is not "someone to be afraid of" but "the ground of being" who is "inherently, objectively, and concretely on our side."[12] This, in turn, opens up the final element of God's inherent narrative of virtue, which allows us to confront cultural pluralism in a way that does not automatically repel the pluralist or relativist. We will discuss in the next chapter.

For now, I would like to conclude with the following observation. In our evangelistic preaching and teaching, I have seldom seen much emphasis placed on the Trinity. If it is even mentioned, it is treated as a doctrine of trivial importance. But most of the time, we don't even touch on it.

For example, a look at the evangelistic sermons institutionally scripted for lay preachers presents us with two sermons: "Who is God?" And "If God is Good, Why So Much Suffering?"—both of which are excellent opportunities to introduce God's ontology of love and tie it to his essential community of being. Yet, neither sermon touches on the doctrine of the Trinity. As a result, its exploration of God's love remains shallow, and it fails to provide the culture with the foundational building blocks for experiencing his heart.

As mentioned already, these distinctions will become more essential as posthumanism marches on. For Mark Zuckerberg, advances in AI and spatial computing are meant to bring us closer together and undo the distance that 2 dimensional screens impose on us. Why does this matter to the Meta CEO? Because his dream from the very start is littered with the fingerprints of God—a dream to connect us all in deeper and richer ways. And yet, the technology has so far done the opposite, contributing to a loneliness epidemic previously unheard of. But it is here that God's communal heart, used as a template for creations very design, can become the balm our alienated culture desperately needs. A theology of togetherness for a disconnected age.

I would like to challenge our evangelistic culture to emphasize the Trinity in its proclamation—not as a dizzying exercise in "heavenly math" (as I heard one preacher put it) but as God's essential community of being, giving us the grounds for embracing his ontology of love. This, I contend, can give the doctrine a level of meaning that interacts beautifully with the absurdity of life. Here, in this strange Hebraic idea, we find a relational origin to the cosmos and consequently, a relational purpose to all that life is.

Thus, in the midst of agony and perplexity, as we meditate on the seasons in which suffering knocks on the door of our lives and on the nights in which the universe mocks our desire for something more—in those moments best captured in what Bob Bennet referred to as "dancing" in "the middle of this madness . . . though I'm not sure why,"[13] we can pause and consider the fact that maybe all begins and ends in an eternal heart of communal love.

# NOTES

[1]  The School of Life, "Søren Kierkegaard."

[2]  "Søren Kierkegaard."

[3]  Steven Gambardella, "The Power of Schopenhauer: A philosophy for life that prizes beauty and compassion."

[4]  Nick Thune, "Nick Thune Standup."

[5]  Hemnant Mehta, "On the Tonight Show, Comedian Nick Thune Joked About What He'd Say As a Christian Youth Pastor."

[6]  Cassidy Robinson, "American Christianity is Shallow."

[7]  William Thomas, "What is Objectivism?"

[8]  Stanford Encyclopedia of Philosophy, "Hume on Religion."

[9]  Paul O'Donoghue, "If God is an underachiever, should we try to help out?"

[10] Ty Gibson, "Seeing the World Through Love-Colored Glasses."

[11] Phillip Ball, "Will We Ever . . . Understand Quantum Theory?"

[12] Richard Rohr, "Love Needs a Face."

[13] Bob Bennet, "Madness Dancing."

CHAPTER 7:

# WITHNESS

---

*"If there's a God, why'd he make me?*
*All of these flaws is all that I see."*
**–Illenium and Call Me Karizma**

The ontological self-abandonment of God reveals that God is far from the self-interested being that many religionists have made him out to be. Instead, God is other-centered. Yet, this very revelation drives us toward an ethereal riddle that transcends our material inhibitions.

In this mystery, we discover that God is three and yet one, a singular-plurality, a simultaneity of individuality and community. Though uncanny, this vision alone provides us with the foundation for divine other-centeredness—for apart from the Trinity, the most one could say of God is that he is loving. However, scripture goes beyond this to affirm that he is the very essence of other-centered love who has existed for all eternity, in the synchronicity of "oneness" and "otherness" (John 10:30).

The next step in our exploration of God is to plunge into the historical application of what has, up to this point, been primarily metaphysical. That is, how does the doctrine of the Trinity value the absurdity of life's daily incoherence and trauma? It is at this point that we need to combine God's ontology and essence into a narrative of virtue that can both sway meaningfully with our chaos and redefine our prosperity. This leads us into a conversation I have engaged countless times, in which the seeker first encounters the historical God of scripture. That is, rather than mere intellectual and philosophical deliberations of Christian theology, God's narrative of virtue is essentially the story of God's heart in motion through the daily angst of life.

This is the stage of the journey in which we begin to unravel exactly what God is like and how his story steps into ours and ours into his. We move away from theology and all of its abstractions and step into chronology and all of its tactility. As the seeker sees God's story step into their own story, the very act beckons their heart to move with him and engage him in a rhythmic back and forth, a divine-human cogitation that is as transcendent as it is immanent. We will now explore this briefly by turning our attention to God's inherent narrative of virtue.

## God's Inherent Narrative of Virtue

In the previous chapters, we explored two main ideas or "postures": *God as inherent and God as virtue*. The next step, however, is to ask what narrative his inherence and virtue communicate to us. So far, we have seen that this is best approached via the Trinity because in this doctrine, we are given the most essential building blocks of God's character and essence—*love and community*. But now we bring this all together by moving from this abstract idea of God and into the experiential invitation that affects our lives in real, tangible ways.

Once again, an exploration at this level is necessarily specific, so for the remainder of this chapter, I will share how I introduce God's inherent narrative of virtue to the seekers I interact with in my particular secular context. Keep in mind that you must incarnate in whatever context you occupy and adjust accordingly—sometimes even from person to person. In my context, the most effective way of engaging secular sojourners with the story of God's heart is to focus on three simple outflows of that heart in real-time. The first is God's altruism, the second is his differentiation, and the third his "uncomfortable *withness*."

## God's Altruism

God's altruism is explored through one simple question: why on earth do you exist? This universal question plunges us into what Italian philosopher Nicola Abbagnano refers to as "the investigation of the meaning of [b]eing"—an act that is "continually faced with diverse possibilities."[1]

In an existential and secular sense, why a person exists is a question with multiple possibilities. No single resolution exists. Therefore, it is up to the individual to determine which path to traverse. Thus, for some, the journey naturally leads toward humanism or nihilism, for others theism or atheism. For many others, it emerges as an eclectic mosaic or bricolage of ever-changing options.

The impact of postmodernity amplifies this "diversity of possibility." But more to the point, it facilitates a negative reaction toward any idea that claims to be supreme in the quest for meaning. Thus, the traditional evangelistic approach in which other perspectives are discounted on the one hand and serenely ridiculed on the other (truth as stagnant) is a sure way to repel the secular explorer.

Consequently, rather than discount or compete with the "diversity of possibilities" I enter the conversation from within it and trust the Holy Spirit to lead the seeker to a faith-driven conclusion (truth as flow). This allows the journey to proceed without threat, but it also exemplifies and models the very perspective on God that I want the seeker to experience: his disinterested, selfless concern for the well-being of the other—his altruism.

Why on earth do I exist? The question has many layers of meaning and is often amplified by dissatisfaction, disillusionment, and suffering. Musical artists Illenium and Call me Karizma echo this in their cynical romantic song "God Dammit" with the question, "If there's a God, why'd he make me?"[2]—a question the poet finds difficult to navigate in light of his "flaws." But when we peel the layers back, we find that there are only three options within the God-possibility.

1.  The first is that we exist because God accidentally created us, or as the deists would say, he "wound up the clock" and left it to tick on its own. These perspectives are so far removed from the narrative of the scriptures that we can lay them aside in the biblical exploration.

This leaves us with only two other options within the biblical interactive model, in which God appears supremely interested in the affairs of men.

2.  The first of these two reasons for our existence in this interactive picture of God is that God *needs* us. Perhaps we were made to be slaves, tasked with performing some menial thing that God couldn't be bothered engaging with. Or perhaps we exist because God was lonely and needed company. Or perhaps we exist because God needed a race

of sentient beings through whom he could stroke his ego through demands for worship and adoration.

As ridiculous as these notions appear, they are not too far from the kind of God that most Christians present to the culture, especially when we use the posture of *God as a claim* in our evangelistic messaging. Phrases such as "We exist to worship God" or "God alone is worthy of worship" or "God made you to worship him"—even the popular mantra "it's all about Jesus, he alone is worthy, etc."—are interpreted by the secular mind as "God is an egotistical child who created an entire world to worship him and when we fail to comply he has a hissy-fit and drowns people."

Or, as one of my own secular friends said to me, "God apparently made us so that we could turn around and lick his toes. And if we don't, he burns us in hell."

However, the Biblical narrative presents a more beautiful, nuanced, and complex picture of divine-human interaction. Here we discover a God who existed for all eternity in a community of agape love. Such a being would never be lonely. Likewise, such a being would never require anything. Thus, the Psalmist quotes God's comical overview for his need of men:

> If I were hungry, I would not tell you, for the world is mine, and all that is in it (Psalm 50:12).

Paul the Apostle emphasizes this point when he writes:

> The earth is the Lord's, and the fullness thereof (1 Corinthians 10:26).

The prophet Moses attested to the same in (Deuteronomy 10:14) when he wrote:

Behold, to the LORD your God belong the heavens, even the highest heavens, and the earth and everything in it [an idea once again expressed in David's poetic excerpt] he stretches out the heavens like a tent (Psalm 104:2).

But perhaps my favorite is found in scripture's most existential book, where God asks its main character Job, "Who has given to Me that I should repay him? Everything under heaven is Mine" (Job 41:11).

In the same sense, the God of scripture transcends the physical universe, meaning that there is nothing in our realm of existence too difficult for him because its limitations do not bind him. [3] Therefore, the idea that God created us to fulfill some task he doesn't want to do is easily dismissed. In the same breath, we can discount the notion that God created us to stroke his ego, for according to the physician Luke, "human hands can't serve his needs—for he has no needs" (Acts 17:25).

To the contrary, Luke adds,

He himself gives life and breath to everything, and he satisfies every need. (25)

Therefore, the notion that humanity exists in any way to offer something to God he does not already possess is faulty. God is love—perfect love—and has no need. We do not exist to stroke his ego, for perfect love has no ego. The apostle Paul defines this love as "not self-seeking" but always other-seeking (1 Corinthians 11:5). Thus, God is, in the fullest sense, altruistic. His acts are always other-centered. Therefore, if God did not create us to *take* something from us, we are left with only one logical possibility:

3. God created us to *give* something to us.

What would an eternal being who is love in his ontology and community in his essence want to give to a temporal creation? If you exist, according to scripture, it is because God created a self-directed and autonomous consciousness to freely offer something to you. What could this be? When these questions are laid before the secular seeker, amazing things happen.

In this stage of the journey, the altruism of God emerges in this simple revelation—that we exist to be recipients of a God who is love. He created us to give us himself: *love*—not love as sentiment, for God is more than mere sentiment, and not love as energy, for God is more than mere energy. *Love as consciousness*. Love as being. Love as an act. This is the love that God, in eternal community, has always been. And in the act of creation we emerge from his imagination into historical reality to be partakers of eternal love and from that love to forge a society that operates according to the divine rhythm of other-centeredness. The God-possibility thus introduces us to this radical idea—that we exist, not to *do* but to *be* and to *be* recipients of self-abandoning love.

### God's Differentiation

The introduction of this idea naturally leads people to recoil to some degree. It is too pure, too free, and can come across as potentially too good to be true. Here, I emphasize God's differentiation.

Differentiation, according to psychologist Dr. David Schnarch, "[is] the dynamic process through which you can live in proximity to a partner and still maintain a separate sense of self."[4]

Therefore, the differentiation of God means that God is capable of affirming his virtue without dependence on other people to do it for him. Differentiation simply means that a conscious being recognizes his or her value irrespective of the affirmation of another.

In human relationships, for example, non-differentiated people often leech significance and meaning from the people around them. We see this in those friends who can't remain single and jump from one relationship to the next, or in codependent parent/child relationships. In these scenarios, people lack differentiation—they are unable to affirm their existence and instead need others to constantly approve of them. God has no such need. He does not need us to stroke his sense of self-importance. On the contrary—God affirms his own existence. Thus, John 12:28 records a conversation between God the Father and God the Son in which the Son says to the Father, "Father, glorify your name!" To which the Father responds, "I have glorified it, and will glorify it again."

This is an example of God's differentiation in scripture. He does not need us to glorify him, in the sense that he derives his sense of self by perpetually inhaling our adoration. God glorifies himself. In the same vein, he has created us to be autonomous beings who justify our existence independent of any created entity. You and I were brought into reality to partake in the eternal love of God. This makes us infinitely and irreplaceable valuable. No amount of trauma, angst, or rejection can ever erode this.

Failure to recognize the differentiation of God leads to errors not only in our evangelistic proclamation (which tends to focus on God as necessity and claim) but also in our practical Christian living. For example, when dealing with the topic of lust, many well-meaning preachers will say "when you lust after a woman (for example) you devalue her. When you are tempted to lust, remember that this woman is someone's daughter, sister, mother, etc. How would you like it if someone did that to your daughter . . . ?"

The tragedy with this view is that in attempting to elevate the value of the objectified woman, the preacher has unintentionally devalued her. How so? By attaching all of her meaning to others, the preacher insinuates that a woman's value is derived from these others. However, this is not the case. The woman is of value, not because she is a daughter, mother, sister, or friend, but simply because she is she. Nothing more! Her value is not dependent but inherent. This is the same point we are making about God. God is a differentiated being—he does not mine his meaning from what he can provide (God as necessity) or from what humans offer him. God is worth knowing because, like you and me, he has an inherent value that affirms itself.

Thus, to bring home the point, we make it clear that we do not exist to feed God's ego. Rather, we exist to be the recipients of his ontological being and to dance with a reality that was designed to reflect the rhythm of other-centeredness. Therefore, all of our worship and adoration is an act of other-centered love, not a ritual coerced by an ego-driven creator.

### God's Uncomfortable *Withness*

So far, we have seen two basic points that communicate one central idea:

1.  We exist to be in relationship with God

2.  We do not exist to affirm God's existence as if he needed us.

Together, both these ideas paint a picture of a God who is relationally other-centered—a being who truly values our individuality and created us uniquely to experience his being in diversity. This idea redefines our existence from one of doing to one of being. It redefines how we interpret our suffering as well as our life's trajectory by providing us with the most foundational and fundamental element of existence: community with the divine. However, what does this community look like? Is it an abstract sensory experience? Is it a rational, cognitive one? Or is it something more?

Because God created us for relationship and other-centered love, then God's presence in our lives is necessarily historical. You cannot be in an other-focused relationship from a distance. Nearness, withness, and immanence are all required. Thus, in this part of the journey, I introduce the seeker to the Sabbath.

In traditional Bible studies, one would never do this. You first have to deconstruct the theological assumptions people bring from their denominational upbringing before entering into a discussion on Sabbath. However, modern secular people generally have no denominational upbringing. Many have never set foot in a church. Therefore, there is no prior commitment or structure that needs to be dismantled. They are seeing the Sabbath for the first time, and in my experience, I have never had any push-back from secular people—to the contrary, they tend to really like the Sabbath.

This is another tragedy that we continue to perpetuate in our evangelistic preaching. Our sermons introduce the Sabbath in an apologetic sense—complete with a list of assumed anti-Sabbath contentions that we answer one by one. These contentions, however, hardly exist in the post-church society in which we currently reside.

As we proudly demonstrate our answers to these questions, we miss the opportunity to present the Sabbath in a truly meaningful and non-reactionary way.

Now, because I discuss the Sabbath in more detail in a future chapter, I wont say too much. But the Sabbath, when introduced as as a narrative marker that reveals God's historical presence in the human story (not a law or command that everyone must keep or else you get the mark of the beast) has a lot of potency in secular missiology. Not only has he made man intimately and personally, but now he sets a day apart to be with them. He is a God of withness—present in the unfolding of life's events.

In light of these foundations, I gently emphasize the most countercultural aspect of God: his uncomfortable *withness*. What is meant here is that God is not simply with us as some friendly coach to enable our best life now. On the contrary, God is "with" as a companion, yes, but an autonomous one. This introduces us to a God who is active and who communicates with content that may at times affirm us and at times offend us.

A historical God, a God with autonomy, cannot be forced into a box with presets. While the modern god of energy ('the universe' being the most popular) may be appeal to a culture that wants to believe in something greater without committing to it, a God of energy cannot interact with the absurdity of being. And yet, this is precisely what the God of scripture does. He is, as Mr. Beaver noted in CS Lewis *'The Lion, the Witch, and the Wardrobe*, "the Lion, the great Lion."[5]

He cannot be tamed. Furthermore, he has an identity, a personality, and a self. He interacts with intention, has ideas and self-knowledge. As a result, for God to have relational value, He must be capable of acting on His values and interests. He cannot be a shadow of human desire but rather a self-governing and self-legislating entity. This means that God has the capacity to debate, to appreciate the perspective of the other, and to—in times of need—relentlessly annoy us.

As desirable as a god who simply affirms us—an energy or essence in the cosmos that we can tap into to acquire the desired outcome and forget when convenient—the truth is relationships are only valuable when there is tension, wrestling, and an uncomfortable withness that exposes and irritates. Outside of this, all you have is a product you can use. Within it, you have a relationship that, when regulated through healthy interdependence, can drive you toward your true humanity.

As mentioned in the previous chapter, our evangelistic series often skip this picture of God. We are consumed by religious jargon that sound fake. Thus, in many of our sermons, God is simply explored in terms of majesty, sovereignty, or glory—all perspectives that, while true, are meaningless in a secular culture and consequently fail to connect with the western mind. I am not saying that we ought to abandon these perspectives of God, but simply that they should not form the basis for how we introduce him to our contemporary, disenchanted world.

Scripture also affirms a God who wrestles, who values man's rational capacity, who weeps and regrets, waits and acts, speaks and listens, and who is an ever-present, historical friend whose acts can be discerned and, at times, resented. The biblical characters understood this autonomous God evidenced by scenes such as

Abraham debating with God (Genesis 18:16-23), Jacob wrestling with him (Genesis 32:22-32), Job and David questioning him (Job 7:20, Psalm 13), and even Jesus—God in human flesh—tasting doubt in his darkest hour (Matthew 27:46).

God's uncomfortable withness means that he is love—true love—and as such he will neither manipulate nor be manipulated, coerce nor be coerced, determine nor be determined. Rather, his identity is separate and secure (as is ours), and his invitation is to engage him in an interdependent relationship in which we experience his active presence in our lives, a presence that can at times call us to new seasons despite the comfort of the old, and new heights despite our familiarity with the depths.

All of this boils down to a simple exploration of God that connects and challenges the secular mind. God is ontologically love—a community of being—and his story is inherently and autonomously virtuous. When we encounter him, we encounter, not an absent God, but one who is ever-present. He invites us to journey with him authentically, embracing the uncomfortable withness that comes from daily walking with his historical, self-validating heart.

But make no mistake, the beauty of God's withness is also the very reason why mankind prefers to erect its own god's. God's who will meet our needs, provide us with benefits, and shape the world in our image without any relational reciprocity intended. And in a world of increasing inequality and injustice, a God of withness, who resists our agendas, advocates for the marginalized and protests economic injustice, is not welcome. This world prefers a digital pharaoh and a quantum Zeus who will enhance the power of empire, elevate the privilege of the elite, and further alienate mankind from its creator. And yet, so much of our preaching paints a picture of a God perfectly at home in the halls of human power. One who does not challenge and call forth the injustice and marginalization of our finest systems and institutions. One who calms our anxieties with pretty Psalms, but hides his voice when racial disparity and systemic injustice are on display.

The withness of God is the protest. It introduces man to a God unlike the gods of its own design. One who will not be edited, or templated, or co-opted for our own imperial designs. One who will rage against the systems of injustice that maintain disharmony and imbalance in our communities and homes.

As I close this chapter, I want to call our evangelism toward a deeper and more meaningful exploration of God's eternal heart. An exploration so captivating that emerging generations, surrounded by technological wonder and power, will be able to easily discern the beauty of Creator above all the mesmerizing capabilities of quantum AI's and its quasi-miraculous capabilities. To this end, we must work to give our world a solid foundation of who God is, to offer them a meaningful conceptualization of existence, chaos, and meaning within the parameters of a maker who is not simply romantically relational, but historically so.

And in doing so, to anchor a new generation in a picture of God that resists us, and is at war with us, in the moments where our political agendas take precedence over love. This is a picture far too divine, too sacred, and too relational for AI, or whatever new gods we will think of, to ever replicate. And it is this picture that our world desperately needs.

His heart is the truth for our time.

# NOTES

[1]  Nicola Abbagnano, "Existentialism."

[2]  God Damnit lyrics © Kmr Music Royalties Ii Scsp, 8 Bit Monster, CALLMEKARIZMA LLC

[3]  Isaiah 40:28.

[4]  David Schnarch, "How To Grow Up: The road map for becoming an authentic adult is also a blueprint for putting passion back in relationships."

[5]  CS Lewis, *The Lion, The Witch, and the Wardrobe*.

CHAPTER 8:

# CREATION

---

*"The secret of living well is not in having all the answers, but in pursuing unanswerable questions in good company."*
**–Rachel Naomi Remen**

The topic of creation is arguably the most difficult to address regarding secular outreach. On the one hand, the culture's prosaic embrace of the theory of evolution means that most people simply accept it as a common matter of fact. While this leads some to the fringes of nihilism, many others turn to Humanism for a more enthusiastic foundation for life.

On the other hand, the culture seems weary of the creation-evolution debates. In fact, scientists are generally encouraged not to debate creationists so that they do not "[give] creationism a scientific legitimacy that it isn't entitled to."[1] To make matters worse, Christians are generally perceived as anti-science. [2] Because Adventists have historically affirmed a literal six-day creation account, we are already at a disconnect the moment the conversation begins.

The impact of postmodernity and its emerging metamodern epilogue has done little to assuage this conceptual clash. In contrast books written by New Atheist icons such as Richard Dawkins, Christopher Hitchens, and Sam Harris emerged as bestsellers during a time when the primary cultural theory was purported to be steeped in relativism.[3]

Likewise, today's heroes of Christianity are not evangelists or preachers like Spurgeon, Whitefield, or Billy Graham but philosophers and apologists like William Lane Craig, Alistair McGrath, John Lennox, and Alvin Platinga. It appears, therefore, at least from a bird's-eye view, that despite the pluralism that surrounds us, questions of origin, especially as they relate to the scientific theory of evolution, still play a significant role in society.

This reality forces us to ask, how can we engage secular sojourners in the story of creation in a way that is meaningful rather than combative? In my experience, I have found, as is often the case, that engaging this theme effectively has less to do with propositions, airtight contentions, and formulas and more to do with posture. In other words, people are open to considering alternative ideas, so long as the ideas are presented in a way that does not clash with their language of being.

After all, one helpful element of postmodern influence is the idea that all truth propositions—including scientific ones—are ultimately socially constructed. No one, not even the physicist or biologist, can stake a total claim on the truth; thus, everyone has a voice at the table. However, as mentioned above, what people reject are ideas presented with condescending and presumptuous attitudes.

Accordingly, *how* we approach this question is of greater significance to the secular mind than *what* we say about the question altogether.

When Adventists approach this topic with the posture of truth as stagnant, presenting with a fundamentalist orientation, weaponizing the Genesis account, demonizing the scientific community, and appealing to pseudoscientific ideas to impose our perspective upon the seeker, the battle is officially lost. Sadly, it appears many conservative Adventists would rather win an argument (or at least feel like they did) and lose a soul than humble themselves long enough to authentically engage the seeker. In this sense, the tensions surrounding modern theories of origin and the Biblical account are unnecessarily inflamed. Once this occurs there is very little chance that the conversation will go anywhere meaningful.

However, when I approach the conversation from the perspective of truth as flow, a different response emerges. Thus, for the remainder of this article, I will share exactly how I engage creation in my particular context with a posture that opens doors rather than closes them and invites continued investigation. To that end, I always engage the seeker with the aim of collapsing distances rather than enhancing them, followed by an exploration of creation as overflow and finally, the essential "what" creation presents to the human experience.

In this chapter, we will deal with "Collapsing Distances" and turn to the other elements in the next chapter.

## Collapsing Distances

The absurdity of life is the core through which we can approximate a working understanding of the secular mind. We have explored this perspective from the beginning as a way of being in the world, an existence that attempts to make sense of the human cry for significance in the face of a frigid universe indifferent to that cry. In this sense, the secular mind is born into a toneless reality where life is despairingly meaningless, leaving you with two options: embrace the emptiness or rage against it with the end goal of creating the meaning that life itself has failed to give you.

As believers, we see this way of being as a tragedy, but to the secular mind it is not necessarily so. After all, the thing we claim provides us with significance, secular culture perceives as coercive. The belief that there is a God, for example, has been used historically to control, manipulate, and monetize guilt.[4] Thus, God is not something that secular people are thirsting after but rather run from.

In this sense, Nietzche's death of God is more of a relief than a catastrophe, and those who embrace it are truly free to self-determine a meaningful life without primordial myths to obstruct them. Yes, the absence of God robs us of ultimate meaning, but with it, human beings can navigate the absurdity and suffering from existence by relying on their own autonomy and investing in their self-advancement as the only truly reliable foundation for a positively consequential life.

Within this tension, evolution emerges as the best possible theory of origin, even if the secular contact retains certain misgivings. To appeal to the faith of pre-moderns is, therefore, to rob the secular man of a belief that sets him free from what political theorist Thomas Paine referred to as "the tyranny [of] religion."[5]

He may indeed hold a certain demur toward science and the reliability of reason, but it's much better than the compulsive corridors of institutionalized religion. Thus, to the secular mind, the scientific view of origins remains influential despite its weaknesses. However, not all secular people stand ready to defend the tenets of Darwinism; equally true is that many secular people simply don't care about the topic at all. The transition from modern rationalism to postmodern relativism and now partway back in the metamodern oscillation between modernity and postmodernity means that many assume evolution is true because it's taught, but do not derive any existential significance from it. It's just there, and that is it. However, this doesn't mean we can discount or ridicule it. Instead, we need to understand it and seek to diminish the distance between our faith and the culture's approach to science.

To that aim, I want to spend a few moments exploring the overarching way in which science works, with a special focus on origins. In doing so, I hope to provide the reader with a bird's-eye view of the conversation, which can give us the insights and tools necessary to engage meaningfully with our secular contacts. I will not attempt to resolve any of the tensions within the debate, but simply offer the model I use. This model, while not designed to answer all questions, is imperative if we wish to keep the conversation going instead of scaring the contact away. To best understand the model, I will begin by exploring the overarching philosophy of science known as methodological naturalism.

## Methodological Naturalism

The theory of evolution assumes methodological naturalism. In the scientific community, methodological naturalism is the *a priori* assumption that the universe is purely natural. That is, there is no supernatural. The American astronomer Carl Sagan put it best when he stated:

The Cosmos is all that is or ever was or ever will be.[6]

As a result, everything that is and could be must of necessity be entirely natural. With this assumption, science embarks on a mission to understand the universe and our world. Rather than saying, "We don't know how birds sing—only God understands it," the scientist says:

> We don't know how birds sing, so we will use this scientific method (encased in methodological naturalism) to study the phenomenon over and over again until we know.

Thus, methodological naturalism is a dome within which science resides. Everything within the dome is physical. Everything beyond the dome is metaphysical. Consequently, science cannot be used to explore the metaphysical because, as far as science is concerned, there is no metaphysical (nothing beyond the dome). Therefore, science is bound to always function within the dome—the assumption that all is natural and material in our spatio-temporal realm. Understanding this "dome" (methodological naturalism as the constraint within which science operates) is imperative to anyone who seeks to engage in this topic with any level of significance.

Creation, on the other hand, is a revealed account. It communicates to us something that inherently involves God. Where methodological naturalism operates on the assumption that there is no God, the creation account operates on the assumption that there is and thus introduces what the dome does not permit—the presence of the metaphysical. In creation, there is no "dome" that constrains our exploration of being. No barrier prevents entry into the supernatural. On the contrary, we are invited to go beyond the natural and experience beyond.

Therefore, creation is about more than our material universe. It transcends this by centering itself in the person of a transcendent God. As a result, a story emerges in creation that differs widely from evolution. Creation is the product of intentional engineering, not blind purposeless forces, and this changes everything. An eternal, meta-temporal consciousness with personality and desire has birthed us. From that intentional birthing, the believer discovers divine origins.

As such, while science tells us we evolved from a lower life form, creation tells us we emerged from the highest life form—complete, personalized, and wanted. Thus, in the end, they are two separate stories in terms of their surface elements and details. Therefore, the question emerges—how do we engage the culture with a completely alternative story of the cosmos that embraces the very things that science is designed to discount as it operates within its dome?

We have three options. First, to deny science as a reliable source of truth and insult its dependability. This is the route that most secular people feel all Christians—particularly the seven-day creationists—affirm. However, the fact that science—within the bounds of methodological naturalism—has been able to advance the most impressive technological revolutions known to man means that ridiculing it is a sure way of ridiculing yourself.

Most secular people think of the failure of religion in terms of bloodshed, social injustice, and primitive superstitions. But science, for all its foibles, has a track record of success from the GPS that gets you to work, the cell phone that connects you with your international relatives, and the medical advancements that give sight to blind children and a greater life expectancy to our species. Thus, understanding the basic way in which science works, even within its naturalistic constraints, and affirming that way, is extremely valuable in conversation. Many times, a secular person will ask you questions about these things just to gauge your response. The vibe you introduce in your answer can be the difference between a continued exploration or the end of the road.

The second option that we have is to redefine our theology to accommodate the discoveries of science. But this has a few problems associated with it. For example, science is always adapting and evolving. Even the theory of evolution has undergone three massive overhauls in recent decades. Thus, if we make the Bible dependent on science, we naturally make science the interpretive moderator of scripture—and an unstable one at that. Thus, while science can certainly enhance our reading of scripture, we encounter problems with an accommodationist approach that elevates a thing within a dome as the infallible interpreter of a thing without a dome. This, to the perceptive reader, is bound to be fraught with difficulties.

The final option, which I recommend, is to allow science to remain within its dome and celebrate its achievements there. I don't go to war with methodological naturalism because the bottom line is: it works! Through it, science has been able to advance in leaps and bounds—a progress not possible if we attributed every mystery to divine power, as the pre-moderns did. Thus, I begin with the perspective that science is good, and the dome is good.

However, I also affirm another contention: while science operates well within the dome, creation calls us beyond the dome into a scenario that transcends the very laws that govern the spatial realm within the dome. As a result, there will always be tensions between science and scripture. One is constrained to function only within the dome. The other transcends the dome. The two, therefore, will never be able to fully harmonize.

The thing within the dome will never be able to prove the thing beyond the dome because the thing within the dome cannot perceive anything beyond it (because, according to the dome, there is no beyond). Likewise, the thing beyond the dome will never fit neatly within the constraints imposed by the dome because it naturally transcends them. Therefore, while the dome is good in that it enables science to advance in ways previously unimaginable, the dome itself can never be used to fully explain or understand the thing beyond the dome—that is, God and the miraculous creation narrative of Genesis 1–2.

Thus, in summary, the presence of the dome in science and its absence in revelation means that scripture and science will never fully harmonize, and that's OK. They aren't meant to. One gives us our metaphysical origins, and the other allows us to understand our spatial-temporal realm by removing the meta-physical as a cop-out to material realities we don't comprehend.

In this sense, you are not trying to resolve the tensions between science and creation. Instead, you are simultaneously embracing the tensions, admitting their difficulty, and honoring both. By staying away from the typical fundamentalist weaponization of Genesis (which always involves the demonization of the scientific community) and assuming a modest bearing, we can engage the secular mind in a way that affirms what they value without attacking it, and simultaneously introduce God's self-revelation without shying away from the tensions between science and faith.

The moment you assume the position that you don't have all

the answers, that you recognize the value of science and are not always sure how to harmonize it with the revelation of scripture, and that you affirm the revelation of scripture with a sense of awe and unpresuming reverence, you will find most secular people respond with respect and engage in the narrative of creation despite the hang-ups that remain. It is when we pretend to know more than we do (like that guy who saw one DVD on geology and now thinks he has a PhD) that we inflame the conversation and damage our witness.

The short version of all of this is that we simply need to be humble in how we approach this discussion. In my personal experience, this posture has enabled me to explore the meaning and beauty of the creation narrative without redefining it. I have yet to interact with a post-modern that is curious about God and simultaneously rejects any and every mention of creation. Most who embrace evolution embrace it as the best possible explanation we have right now, not as an absolute truth.

Others have a non-committal relationship with it and accept that once a supernatural being becomes a variable in reality, it inherently alters our conceptualization of everything we claim to know. But it's equally true that emerging generations don't care about the evolution debate like their fathers did. And of those who do, a posture of humility goes a long way to connecting and exploring the narrative of creation with them. You don't need to be an expert in biology to have a meaningful interaction to the narrative of creation, and that's the bottom line.

Nevertheless, it isn't enough to simply affirm the beauty of science. We also need to affirm the beauty of the Genesis story. Contrary to what many assume, it is an extremely sophisticated and complex literary masterpiece. There is so much there that we don't fully understand and perhaps never will. Thus, we approach the Genesis story, not as owners of the story but as recipients of its beauty and grandeur. We hold this narrative high in our hearts, while simultaneously affirming the wonders of the scientific method. To the questions of how we harmonize one with the other, I simply respond, "I don't know."

This approach is built on a process known as "collapsing distances." Rather than arguing how evolution is an idiotic idea, how the scientific community wants to erase God or—as Adventist evangelists commonly do—how evolution emerged because people stopped keeping the Sabbath (seriously?), I propose that it is best to take a deep breath, celebrate the beauty and reliability of science, and do the thing we struggle to do the most as Adventists—admit we don't have all the answers.

And yet, despite our inability to explain all things, we have encountered this self-revelation in scripture, this story of creation that grounds our being and our existence in the midst of life's absurdity and suffering, and that this story—despite all the mysteries—is breathtaking and worth considering. Perhaps no one has expressed the nature of this approach as well as Rachel Naomi Remen, who brilliantly stated,

> The secret of living well is not in having all the answers, but in pursuing unanswerable questions in good company.[7]

At this juncture, we explore the two perspectives: creation as overflow and the essential "what" of the narrative. In these two headings, we will find a poem that interacts so meaningfully with the secular language of being that the endless debates over creation and evolution will seem a little less significant.

# NOTES

[1] "Bill Nye v Ken Ham: should scientists bother to debate creationism?" The Guardian.

[2] Sarah Kropp Brown, "Are Evangelicals Anti-Science?"

[3] Dennis Prager, "Why Are Atheist Books Best Sellers?"

[4] Allen Clifton., "Organized Religion: A Tool for Ignorance, Power, and Control."

[5] Austin Cline, "Insightful Thomas Paine Quotes on Religion."

[6] Daryl E. Witmer, "What if the cosmos is all that there is?"

[7] Rachel Naomi Remen. "My Grandfather's Blessings: Stories of Strength, Refuge, and Belonging" (Riverhead Books, 2001)

CHAPTER 9:

# **OVERFLOW**

*"I want to leave, to go somewhere where I should be really in my place, where I would fit in . . . but my place is nowhere; I am unwanted."*
**–Jean Paul Sartre**

In his debate with Ken Ham, American television presenter Bill Nye opened his remarks by saying, "Here tonight we're going to have two stories. And we can compare Mr. Ham's story to the story from what I will call 'the outside' . . ."[1] In effect, Nye was summarizing the entire creation and evolution debate, with all of its complex variables, down to the bottom line—stories. Creation is a story. Evolution is a story. One is rooted in metaphysical claims, the other does not presume to enter such themes, but it nevertheless provides its student with a diverse narrative of human origins.

Thus, the father of evolution–Charles Darwin himself–could speak of this view of origins as one which contains "grandeur."[2] This perspective was robustly captured by the late historian of science Will Provine when he referred to the concept of "Intelligent Design" as "utterly boring"—a thing he couldn't "even be bothered thinking about anymore."[3] Likewise, in my personal discussions with atheists, the same theme is repeated with some going so far as to say that the notion of evolution is a humbling and exhilarating proposition.

However, "grandeur," "exhilarating," and "humbling" are not the kind of words one would use to describe stoic ideas. Rather, they are reserved to describe the things that touch us on a deeper level—things like stories.

In light of this, I have found it best to engage creation not as a contentious postulation at war with materialistic theories, but as a story that stands on its own beauty. In doing so, I bypass much of the propositional debate and instead invite the seeker to consider the biblical origin story as just that—a story with a plot line that presents us with a narrative of life, self, and destiny fundamentally distinct from modernism's naturalistic claims. In doing so, I am not suggesting one perspective is superior, but rather that they are different approaches. The conviction that will lead a person toward accepting that they came from the heart of God and are, in fact, his work of art is a conviction I leave entirely up to the Holy Spirit.

To this question, some ask- "What do you do when a person demands an exploration that transcends stories?" But to be honest, I have never encountered this scenario. Not only has postmodernism assuaged such dogmatic approaches to the origin of life, but my goal in connecting with secular culture has never been to convince the mind opposed to God to accept God but to journey with the mind that has already encountered God and is searching to put the pieces together. A person on that journey is generally open to alternative viewpoints because the introduction of a supra physical being brings with it a set of variables that automatically alter one's dogma.

However, for those who require a deeper and more detailed exploration of the issues, my advice would be to outsource that part of the journey to ministries and thinkers who are immersed in that space. Once that recommendation has been made, you can invite the seeker to consider the narrative of creation for what it is worth nonetheless, and thus embark on the journey. As mentioned in the previous chapter, once I have collapsed the distance between science and faith through an exploration of methodological naturalism's dome and the metaphysicalism that scripture claims transcends the dome I engage the seeker in two diverse but interlocked perspectives: creation as overflow and the essential "what" of creation.

## Creation as Overflow

The concept of creation as overflow is simple in that it merely takes the narrative of God's heart which we have already begun exploring in the doctrine of God and Trinity, and asks a simple question—why is this God creating?

The question alone is profound. First, the very fact that creation has not always existed but has a beginning at a point in history speaks to the conscious and individual nature of God. If God were merely the energy source from which creation flows, one could posit that creation has co-existed along with God.

Consider the sun, for example. For as long as there has been a sun, there has been light proceeding from the sun. The sun is the source and the rays of light flow from it for as long as it has existed. Similarly, if God were an impersonal source of the universe's existence, one would expect the universe to be as eternal as God himself—proceeding from him for as long as he himself has been.

However, this is not what we see. Instead, contemporary cosmology demonstrates that the universe indeed has a beginning and, in fact, quite possibly an end.

The only plausible explanation in this scenario is that God is a willful being who can decide at what point to bring creation into being. That is, creation does not helplessly flow from him but he, by decision and individual choice, willed to bring it into effect at a certain point in history. Such a proposition negates the "energy god" so popular in modern New Age ideology.

Second, the question brings us back to the Triune nature of God. Because the Bible declares that God is both "love" and "one" we are immediately confronted with a self-contradiction. How can God be both "one" and "love"? Love is other-centeredness. However, if God existed for all eternity as a strict singularity, who was the "other" upon whom he centered? Thus, if God is one, the most we can say is that once he created, he began to love. In other words, God can be loving and one, but he cannot be love and one. Unfortunately, the Bible says that he is one and love, which leaves us in contradiction. That is, of course, until we discover that God is an eternal community of beings who have existed for all eternity in an eternal relationship of agape love within the plurality of his being. In this sense, the Triune nature of God solidifies his ontology of love.

This now leads us back to creation. Why would a God of love create? What would have been his motivation? What purpose would have undergirded our existence? Did God create us because he needed something? We have already seen that this is not the case. Did he create us because he wanted us to do something for him?

We have already seen that this is not the case. Unlike the pagan gods who made man by accident or to accomplish a task they could not be bothered doing themselves, the God of scripture did not design us for any of the above. So then, why did he create us?

By virtue of elimination, we are left with only one alternative. If God did not create us to *get* something from us, then he must, by necessity, have created us to *give* something to us.

God's ontology of love provides us with the "something"—agape love. We can henceforth perceive a God who, in mystery, existed for eternity in a relationship of other-centered love within the plurality of his being. The Father loved the Son and the Spirit. The Son loved the Father and the Spirit. The Spirit loved the Father and the Son. Thus, they are one and love because they are the very essence of other-centeredness—a singular-plurality that has existed for all eternity in a harmonious interpersonal exchange of other-centered passion—this is God. And this God, it appears, came to manifest his love by sharing it.

Thus, we can imagine a moment in time (in our limited human conceptualizations) in which God entered into counsel and chose at that moment to create a universe of sentient beings in his/"our" image. This means that these beings possess autonomy, differentiation, and individuality—all elements that are predicated on freedom of the will. From this foundation, God would have created a new reality in which its inhabitants could freely enter into a mutual and reciprocal exchange with him. A dance in which both parties pour out onto the other—God's love to man and man's love reciprocated back to God—is a divine cacophony of romance, meaning, and beauty.

This perspective, when properly introduced, immediately interacts with the secular language of being, which values autonomy and self-determination. But likewise, it raises many questions. For many, the only picture of God they have ever encountered is narcissistic, dictatorial, and demanding. What are they to do with a being who, according to creation's narrative, made us solely to give to us and not take from us? The imagery is immediately liberating and confronting.

For those who have a smidget of religion to contend with, a complex reordering of their ideological gears begins, and at first, the result is confusion. So much needs to be rethought and revisited that it can almost appear overwhelming. After all, religious culture is predicated on "don'ts" (don't do this, go there, eat that, listen to those, watch these, or be associated with them, so that you will not become as they) and the tragic outcome of this is that God comes to be seen as a demanding being who wants to take everything remotely enjoyable from us because it doesn't make him happy. For those who increasingly have no religious background whatsoever, the proposition that we exist to be the recipients of eternal love flies in the face of everything they have believed to this point—that is that man's existence has no deep meaning, that life is a futile struggle against the indifference of nature on the one hand, or a self-determined opportunity to concoct meaning out of the absurdity on the other.

Suffice to say, this is not a perspective that one can tap on like a tourist rushing through his European holiday. Rather, this is a perspective upon which we must rest, for it confronts the angst of the existentialist, the nihilist, the humanist, the postmodernist, and the posthumanist all in one fell swoop.

To the absurdity of a heart gasping for significance in the face of a universe indifferent to such primordial desires—creation arrives like a tender mother stroking her fingers through her child's hair, whispering soothing poems. To the nihilist declaring that all is nothing, that life is vapid, that pain and suffering are mere banalities and that destiny and meaning are illusions bathed in subjective desire; the narrative of creation is like a father who gives all he has for his daughter, as if to say, "You are worth more than being itself." To the humanist desperately constructing his own meaning by gathering the pieces of existence and grafting them together into an explicated bricolage, the narrative of creation is like a grandmother who motions to her anxious grandson, "come here... rest." To the postmodernist who mocks the naivety of enthusiasm, creation says. "Come and be naive a while." To the posthumanist who rages against extinction by taking control of nature's evolutionary process, creation beckons, "come, and be safe with me."

Creation as overflow is more than a Biblical point to be made, but a profound, soul-healing revelation that can reauthor a person's entire foundations. It amplifies our sense of value, energizes our relationship with the self, and rearranges our entire worldview (even constructing one anew for those who have never had one). To consider for a moment that you exist to be the recipient of divine love and that the universe itself is in motion because an eternal community of agape love chooses to bestow that love upon created beings is powerful enough to reset the why of stars, galaxies, and human consciousness.

"Why am *I*?" asks the heart of man. "To be the recipient of God's eternal love" is creation's answer. What are we to do with such a claim? We can mock its enthusiasm, doubt its avidity, and reject its ardor, but one thing is clear—this story refuses to conform, for it aims to sweep us off our feet, to shock us in the midst of our enlightened intellectualism like a love-struck youth, and laugh amorously at our uptightness and informed rigidity. *Lighten up, won't you?* Is this question etched into those playful eyes that promise both liberation and anxiety. Idyllic and charming, a beauty grounded in its very prose, one that needs not attack, mock, or degrade in order to make up for its supposed deficiency.

No, the narrative of creation is far more than a Molotov cocktail to be thrown at the convoy of naturalistic advancement but rather, a delightful revelation woven into the fabric of scripture by the very voice that beckons us from beyond the dome—a voice that teaches us, bound and incarcerated souls, to dream once more, and to self-liberate our imaginations from the constraints of laboratories and charts into the improbable and perhaps even impossible possibility that we, the crowning act of creation, are just that—beings etched in autonomy and freedom, for one singular purpose—to eternally bathe in the cosmic rays of eternal love for which we were designed and to which we are beckoned from birth to destiny. To this end, we finally have a response to the "nowhere" philosopher Jean Paul Sartre spoke of when, in his search for a place to belong, he concluded that he was "unwanted."[4] Not according to the creation narrative, for there we discover our very existence boils down to this simple proposition: we belong.

Do our evangelistic presentations capture such seduction? Or are we weaponizing creation to instill fear of science, to rage against the very structure that is responsible for the existence of the laptop we are using to produce our PowerPoint presentation, or to profit from its narrative by taking advantage of the occasion to promote our own agenda of Sabbath observance? I cannot speak for every preacher, evangelist or campaign but from what I have seen, creation is a theme we touch on long enough to sneak our Sabbath agenda in, an agenda that we then season with the tantalizing spice of dramatic anti-science discourses that make claims such as there would "never have been an evolutionist"[5] if we all kept the Sabbath. Not to mention the free resource provided by the General Conference evangelism resource center titled, "Don't Let the Monkey Fool You"[6] in which creation is approached as a contra-science perspective, engaged with at a shallow and elementary level only a pre-conditioned fundamentalist would approve of. Then, halfway through the sermon, the entire discourse shifts from an exploration of creation to a sermon on how to have a better marriage. Is this really the best we can do, considering the challenges posed in our contemporary age and the opportunities that beckon us from within the depths of Genesis 1-2? I hope not.

Are there significant questions to explore? Yes. Is creation a historical reality and not merely a wondrous poem with existential value? Yes. However, we begin the journey with its inherent beauty, and from there, we can embark on the messy adventure of appreciating the advancements possible within the dome of methodological naturalism, all while dancing with the tension of a story rooted in what Nye, as quoted above, referred to as from "the outside," a story rooted in the beyond which the dome itself cannot conceive. To develop such an approach in our evangelistic proclamations ought to have been a priority a long time ago.

This brings us to the point of tying it all together in the essential "what" of creation, which we will explore in the next chapter.

# NOTES

[1]  Bill Nye, "Bill Nye Debates Ken Ham – HD (Official)."

[2]  Charles Darwin, On the Origin of Species, p. 490, as quoted in "There is Grandeur in this View of Life."

[3]  Will Provine, Expelled: No Intelligence Allowed (2008, documentary).

[4]  Jean-Paul Sartre, "Albert Camus and Jean-Paul Sartre / Camus and the Death Penalty."

[5]  Ministerial Association, General Conference of Seventh-day Adventists, God's Seal for Survival.

[6]  Ministerial Association, General Conference of Seventh-day Adventists, Don't Let the Monkey Fool You.

CHAPTER 10:

# MEANING

---

*"Those who are devoid of purpose will
make the void their purpose."*

**—Friedrich Nietzsche**

In the previous two articles, we explored a meaningful way to approach creation with an emerging post-church culture. We have seen that in our contemporary age, two approaches to human origin exist. One is the modernist approach, which places its faith in science and its discoveries. The other is the post-modernist approach, which questions the reliability of reason and science and therefore takes a less dogmatic path to questions of human origin. Add to this the emergence of meta-modernity in which modernism and post-modernism begin to approximate one another in a non-rhythmic dance, and you end up with a culture where some embrace evolution on Monday while vacillating on it on Tuesday—a milieu in which the story of human origins is open-ended, with science providing a better alternative to religion for some, and others pursuing a more neo-mythical vision of where we come from and where we are headed.

In this context, Christians should to be prepared to recognize the perspective with which their friends are engaged at any given moment because each perspective requires a different approach. For modernists, an apologetic approach, exemplified by ministries like *The Bible and Beer Consortium* and apologists like William Lane Craig, is essential. For others, apologetics tends to be overkill. In these scenarios, the narrative approach works best.

When it comes to the narrative approach, the best angle is to seek, from the onset, to collapse the distance between the story of naturalism and the story of supernaturalism. We do so by imagining a dome in which naturalism resides and learning to appreciate and celebrate the dome for what it's worth and what it has accomplished. But we also call the sojourner to the world beyond the dome, which scripture assumes from the beginning, and thus demonstrate that once a world beyond the dome is introduced into the story, a whole new plot line can emerge. There are new possibilities, dimensions, and adventures in a universe designed by a conscious transphysical entity. This alters not only our origin story but also our present being and destiny. In short, creation as the overflow of God's love changes everything—it is a story that, if true, demands man's total attention.

However, the journey into creation has not yet ended. Rather, we must move from creation as an overflow to the essential "what" of creation. The meaning here is that we are moving from "why did God create?" to "what purpose is there in my existence?" It is one thing to say that God created us to be the eternal recipients of his love (the why), but where do we go from there? To what aim do we arise in the morning? To what peak do we set our sights? Upon what horizon do we now cast our gaze?

Failure to explore the essential "what" of creation leaves us with an overly romanticized view of origins, in which man appears to wander in bliss like a love-struck teenager who cannot think or function pragmatically in the world. But while God created us to be the recipients of his love (our why), that love is dynamic and intelligent, not static and fanciful. This means that God's love is to be pictured, not as two inamoratas aimlessly staring into each other's eyes, but as partners moving together into purpose. There is adventure, story, growth, development, and meaning here—a universe created to be explored, traversed, and investigated to its utter depths. A pursuit of answers and insights into the bottomless, meta-cosmic reality that is God's heart. This, I refer to as the essential "what" of creation.

## The Essential "What" of Creation

Why we exist is a powerful question that touches both the joys and agonies of life. To love and be loved is the answer. However, as already stated, if not coupled with an essential understanding of what creation entails, this answer can rapidly degrade into a cliché with little potency in confronting the existential challenges of the age. If creation's reason has any significance, the love it calls us to must transcend mere sentimentalism.

Unfortunately, so much of our preaching presents God's love this way. When we say "God loves you" so much, the proposition loses its momentousness. It becomes a vapid and pallid idea that lacks potency and applicatory power. The essential "what" of creation is, therefore, a perspective I have learned from many conversations with secular seekers who appreciate a faith rooted in God's love but who, nevertheless, are searching for a love that transcends mere colloquialisms—that is, a love that is heuristic and can help make sense of the incongruities of life. Love that materializes into purpose, direction, and motive—three elements without which existence collapses into routine and toxicity. In order to do this, I return to the Genesis account with a simple question: what was man's purpose on earth? The answer to this question is given in Genesis 1:28, where God says, "be fruitful, multiply and replenish the earth."

## Be Fruitful

Friedrich Nietzsche once said, "Those who are devoid of purpose will make the void their purpose."

In other words, mankind was not made to wander. In the absence of purpose, the absence itself becomes an object of pursuit. This gives birth to the emptiness we presently observe; emptiness that the modern mind aims to resist through its modes of navigation. And these modes, while potentially miry, unsatisfying, and convoluted, are, nevertheless, greater than no pursuit at all. All this speaks to the simple reality that our lives are meant to mean—that we were designed with a divine echo that daily whispers, "be fruitful."

This call is deeply embedded in us and provides a foundation to explore, with a fellow seeker, the purpose, motive, and direction of life. The conversation is necessarily vulnerable and, intimately, meaningful. It helps the contact see that, contrary to popular perception, God is not withholding, not coercing, not limiting but to the contrary—calling us to advance, develop and to liberate ourselves from the constraints of insecurities and inhibitions to discover and taste our true purpose as children of infinite mystery.

Herein lies the beauty of the creation narrative, for it provides us with a metaphysical foundation for contending with the absurdity of life. Life is suffering, and this is its most natural state. Were a man to do nothing but wait for nature to act on him, he would suffer. In other words, we do not need to seek out suffering. Suffering is the natural stream of life.

As writer Tom Stevenson once eloquently stated, "pain and anguish [are] woven into the fabric of life."[1] And the only way to contend with this reality is to find, as Nietzsche affirmed, meaning in suffering. So we pursue significance because if we discover virtue in life that outweighs and transcends the suffering, we have found the key to justifying our "pressing on" despite the difficulty of daily existence. The objective is thus, rather than submitting to suffering as victims of its oppressive regime, to dedicate our lives to overcoming, to the path of mastering life, taming its demons, and vanquishing its hordes. In doing so, we rise above the waters that seek to drown us and produce something of meaning—the fruit of mind and being.

**Multiply**

But the Biblical call doesn't end there. It is not simply about living a fruitful life, but about multiplying that fruitfulness. Here we find a foundation for kinship, which we will discuss in much more detail when we touch on the doctrine of the family. For the time being, it will suffice to focus simply on the concept of multiplication, because it gives way to incredibly profound existential questions. Questions such as, If your life as it currently stands were to be multiplied across the earth—would suffering increase or decrease? If your children multiplied your character and choices, in what direction would they move the story of humanity? If your priorities in life were multiplied *en masse,* will our world be more beautiful as a result?

These questions matter for one simple reason. It is easy for us, as self-centered beings, to assume that our decisions do not impact the flow of human history. "What does it matter, so long as I hurt no one?" Can often be translated as, "What does it matter if the damage is minuscule or imperceptible?" Because the truth is, no decision we make is without consequence, but we are often too small-minded to perceive the depth of our choices. Therefore, it is helpful to imagine those choices as being multiplied and to ask what their result in that sense would be. For whatever cosmic significance we may find in their exponential state, we can also find in their daily microstates that impact our consciousness, identity, and personhood.

The purpose of life is, therefore, greater than the transcendence of my individual suffering. It is about whether my method of individual transcendence, if multiplied, would infuse the earth with a greater or lesser degree of collective suffering. Likewise, as per the original design, if I am beautifying the earth through my life, I am called to multiply that beautification and thus make the earth more beautiful. This brings us to the theme of "replenishing."

## Replenish the Earth

We arrive at the final aspect of our essential "what"—to "replenish" the earth. Contrary to what many assume, God did not create a perfectly cultivated world. Instead, he created a perfectly cultivated garden, in which he placed Adam and Eve. But beyond that garden, Genesis 2 tells us that the rest of the earth was uncultivated. This means that Adam and Eve's job was to cultivate the rest of the world. They were to take the beauty of Eden and reproduce it throughout the globe. The invitation to fruitfulness and multiplication is embedded here. There is no way that two people can cultivate and maintain entire continents on their own. Instead, it was through multiplication that their act of beautifying the earth would spread until the entire globe became one giant Eden.

Without going into much more detail (once again reserved for the doctrine of the family) I want to make one major observation. This observation is captured in John Mark Comer's book *Loveology,* in which he brilliantly states that the purpose of Adam and Eve was simple—to make the earth a more beautiful place.

Indeed, we can take the complexity of humanity's essential *what* and bring it down to this singular aim—we exist to be the recipients of God's eternal love. And what does that look like? It looks like a life that perpetuates beauty, an existence that revolves around cultivating the potentiality of the earth, until at last, the entire planet glows as an ecological emerald, a marvel suspended in the cosmos. That is our *what.*

This perspective leads to incredibly compelling conversations. In what way are you making the earth a more beautiful place? In what way are you beautifying the earth through your daily decisions, priorities, patterns, and rituals? Is your pursuit of amusement making the earth a more beautiful place? How about your obsession with duties? Or the escapism offered by the rampant consumerism of the age?

In what way do our lives fulfill their original purpose—to make the earth a more beautiful place? Because so long as we exist outside that purpose, we will always tread toward anger, violence, and despair. Psychologist Jordan Peterson put it this way:

> People who have no purpose in their life are embittered by the difficulties of their life, and they become first bitter, and then resentful, and then revengeful, and then cruel, and there are plenty of places to go past cruel.[2]

Thus, the narrative of creation captures this compelling vision of a humanity created to receive the eternal love of God and to, in turn, live out that love in practical ways that give birth to complex social structures, cultures, and societies that seek to beautify the earth and an individual existence that operates with the aim of being fruitful and multiplying the joy of that fruitfulness across the globe. To imagine an existence governed by such other-centered parameters and to seek to live that existence out in our daily life despite the cruelty of existence is the apex of meaning and value that any man can hope to discover.

Yet, even this heroic act can collapse when confronted by a universe that mocks our greatest accomplishments as meaningless drops of sweat in a vast ocean of repression. But not according to the creation narrative. In this story, we find a vision of human origin, in which man was designed for the very act of quelling the mystery that encompasses him. All of this coalesces into an existential marvel of origins that redefines so much of reality and experience.

And yet, the adventure doesn't end there. Mankinds destiny as a multiplier of beauty, is not confined to a terrestrial boundary. To the contrary, the eden that we cultivate on the earth is meant to adorn the cosmos. I often like asking secular seekers, what would have happened if humanity fulfilled its purpose and replenished the earth? What then? Do we sit back and enjoy and eternal holiday? Or do we put our minds together with the goal of becoming a multiplanetary species, terraforming different worlds, and multiplying eden there as well? In this sense, Elon Musk's vision isn't really that far fetched. Nested within posthumanisms goal of a colony on Mars then, lie the very fingerprints of God.

Thus, I contend that when approached properly, the creation narrative emerges as something fundamentally more compelling than a club to bludgeon modern theories of origin. To the contrary, properly engaged, creation offers us so many answers and mysteries that they suffice to occupy our attention and redefine our lives irrespective of those complex debates.

How tragic, then, that our evangelistic approach rarely taps into this beauty. When I say evangelistic, I am not speaking merely of sermonizing, but also of our Bible study resources and the ways in which we are taught to engage others in the conversation over creation and evolution. Sadly, too many Adventists appear to have blindly followed the evangelical call to arms against modern science and evolution. In doing so, we have weaponized Genesis to such a degree that we can no longer derive nor bestow the beauty contained within its plotline. I contend it's time to slow down, take a step back, and reassess our approach because if we do not, we will continue to ostracize the very culture we have been called to reach.

As I close the portion on creation and absurdity, I hope that the reader can appreciate a bit more the colossal failure of many of our evangelistic approaches to the narrative of creation and perhaps be motivated to help craft a more meaningful and valuable approach that can offer emerging generations a perspective of human origins worth contending with in the face of contemporary incredulity.

# NOTES

[1]   Tom Stevenson, "Does Suffering Make Life Worthwhile?"

[2]   Jordan Peterson, "Jordan Peterson | Full Address and Q&A | Oxford Union" (script).

CHAPTER 11:

# SIMULATION

---

*"What is real? How do you define 'real'?"*

**–Morpheus, The Matrix Film**

I can't conclude our exploration of creation without turning our gaze to the future. Because it turns out, the entire debate over creation and evolution is itself evolving in an entirely new direction which, I believe, will take on a greater role in the next 10-30 years.

In fact, it has already begun.

But first, allow me to set a foundation.

Modernism questioned the source of truth.

Post-modernism questioned the existence of truth.

Metamodernism now questions the narrative we assign to truth.

But the truth wars are about to fade, giving way to a new tension far more complex.

What is real?

In our contemporary age, people no longer inhabit a singular dimension. Instead, we bounce back and forth between two separate dimensions – the physical and the virtual.

Ancient cultures as well as contemporary spiritual/ religious ones are similar in that they inhabit both a physical and meta-physical reality. Worldview is what facilitates this dual-dimensional existence. In the Old Testament, the sanctuary facilitated this experience in that God's temple represented the place where heaven and earth met. And virtually all religious and spiritual societies are rooted in this celestial imagination that sees both the material and the immaterial as co-existing phenomena.

But with the advent of modernity, human beings shifted – for the first time ever – into a mono-dimensional existence. Everything was material and governed by natural law. Nothing more.

This perspective remains, but something new has emerged. With the digital revolution, the secular mind now inhabits a dual dimension once more. Only its not physical and meta-physical. It's physical and virtual. We bounce back and forth between the world governed by the laws of nature and the world on our mobile phones, governed by a different set of laws. In this virtual dimension we can be anyone, go anywhere, and consume anything in ways not possible within the physical realm. This dual-dimensional existence is forming emerging generations into beings whose felt-sense of reality differs from older generations. And with the advancement of virtual and augmented reality (coupled with the prospective success of the metaverse and human-computer integrations like Neuralink), soon these generations will no longer be bouncing back and forth between two alternative dimensions. They will instead exist within both of them at the same time.

What this means is that while modernism, post-modernism, and metamodernism all questioned the nature of truth at varying degrees, what comes next is not so much a question of what is true as much as it is a question over what is real.

In other words, previous philosophical shifts have questioned the nature of truth but have always held to a "shared perspective" for affirming statements about reality. And yet, this very shared perspective is something that dissolves in a world where virtual and physical dimensions overlap permanently. In this new world, reality itself is under question.

## The Simulation Hypothesis

All of this paves the way for a new and previously unheard-of worldview shift that is gaining momentum in the metamodern era: the Simulation hypothesis.

In his Builtin.com article, "What Is Simulation Theory? Are We Living in a Computer Simulation?" tech journalist Mike Thomas writes,

> "Simulation theory says that we are all likely living in an extremely powerful computer program, directed by an entity outside of our physical comprehension. In this situation, humans are not necessarily "real" and tangible beings, but instead predetermined, coded constructs of the digital world we inhabit. Living in a simulation can be likened to living in a gigantic game of The Sims, except we ourselves are the characters inside the screen."[1]

In other words, reality as we know is not really reality. It is a simulated reality like what we experience in a video game. If this is the case, then we humans do not actually live in what Elon Musk refers to as "base reality" but rather, inside of a synthetic, coded, and manufactured reality similar to what we see in the Matrix films.

Thomas supplies a good foundation for understanding where all this has come from when he writes,

> "If we live in a computer simulation, then who is the programmer? Swedish philosopher Nick Bostrom contends in his 2003 paper 'Are You Living in a Computer Simulation?' that future generations might have mega-computers that can run numerous and detailed simulations of their forebears, in which simulated beings are imbued with a sort of artificial consciousness. Odds are, we are products of that simulation, and we may not be the original species of humans."

Whether the Bostrom's Simulation Theory is true, accurate, or even scientific is not something I want to explore here. Plenty has been written on this topic for you to Google to your hearts content. My main interest isn't in the veracity of the theory but in its cultural impact and the implications this raises for mission in a post-human era.

Humanity, it turns out, is shifting back to a dual-dimensional existence. We are not psychologically wired to exist within the confines of western modernism and its rigid commitment to the dome. We instinctively know there is a world beyond the dome. But more to the point, we know that whatever this world is, it is not entirely separate from our own. This enchantment was welcomed in pre-modern generations who saw the world through magic, myth, legend, mythos, and religion. But in modernity, the philosopher Charles Taylor contends, all such enchantment has been taken from us.[2]

That is, until it wasn't. With the arrival of digital and virtual reality, many have begun to ask — if this technology continues to improve until a video game is indistinguishable from reality, then how can we be sure we are not already living in such a game?

The question might seem silly to some. But it strikes at the root of our psychological need for an enchanted existence. Without returning to the pre-modernism that frightens the secular mind, we can nevertheless restore enchantment to existence by postulating that the world we inhabit is a simulated version of the real thing. And if this is the case, then it means there is a simulator (possibly a highly advanced form of artificial intelligence) which means there is a base reality (possibly inhabited by a highly advanced specie of humans) and perhaps even an infinite number of alternative realities simulated across time and space for us to someday explore.

The keen reader will observe something here. But rather than saying it myself, I will simply quote Medium author Nic James who wrote, "The Simulation Theory intersects with religious thought…"[3]

James was being kind. Fellow author Morné Visagie was more direct when he wrote that the simulation hypothesis is nothing more than "a religion for atheists."[4]

Morne goes on to write, "If we live in a simulation, then surely there would need to be a simulator. This sounds a whole lot like a science-fiction version of God."[5]

For this reason, many in the scientific community are rejecting the entire premise as nothing more than pseudo-science. While some like physics academic Melvin Vompson insists he has found evidence for the simulation hypothesis[6], others such as theoretical physicist Sabine Hossenfelder attacks it as "mixing science with religion".[7] The astrophysicist Neil De Grasse Tyson initially supported the theory, giving it a "better than 50-50 odds"[8] but was later convinced otherwise by colleague and professor. J. Richard Gott.[9]

However, this back and forth hasn't prevented simulation theory from gaining steam as a potential alternative to pre-modern and modern cosmologies. Tv and radio presenter Dominik Diamond says he finds "the theory that we are all characters in a huge sim ever more believable – and appealing."[10]

And while its still early stages, the continued advance in AI, augmented reality and virtual reality will, at the very least, lay the necessary groundwork for a new generation to embrace some version of the simulation hypothesis. As the lines between the real and the digital blur more, as our perception of what is grounded and artificial is numbed, and as our collective disenchantment collapses under the weight of life's absurdity, we will have before us a perfect alternative to religion that offers a return to mystery and wonder without the pitfalls of what modernism has deemed mere superstition and ignorance.

How should missional Adventists contend with this possibility? How should we prepare to engage the shift toward what appears to be a post-secular re-enchantment that integrates religion and science, thus meeting the cultures transcendent longings, without any appeal back to pre-modern dogma or religiosity?

Once again, we have to look beneath the feature of simulation hypotheses to discern its benefit. If simulation theory is true, then it means a higher and more advanced specie of humans has crafted the simulation we inhabit. And if this is so, then the nihilist nightmare of postmodernity collapses. No longer do we have to fear extinction, dystopia, or annihilation. Clearly, mankind has progressed to such a degree that not only do we still exist in a higher base dimension, but we have become creators of our own universes.

Once again, the benefit proves to be primordial. Always, beneath the fancy jargon and nerdy dialogue we discover the childlike heart searching for safety and significance. Classical Christianity has failed to offer this to the world. So now, the world seeks to engineer it for itself.

And in the midst of this, some Christians are working hard to get ahead of the curve and engage the culture at its own philosophical shifts. The Global Architect Institute, for example, has entered the conversation from both a Biblical and technological angle with a radical proposal: *Simulation Creationism.*

According to their website,

> "Simulation Creationism is a belief that combines traditional Creationism with the Simulation Theory. It posits that the universe and life are the result of specific acts of creation by a higher power, but within a simulated reality. This advanced simulation is designed and maintained by an intelligent creator, blending the religious notion of a divine being with the technological concept of a virtual universe. It maintains Creationism's core idea of purposeful divine creation, while integrating the hypothesis of our universe being an artificial,

technologically-generated construct, offering a unique intersection of spirituality and scientific speculation."

Some may look at such a project as mere syncretism where scripture is redefined according to whatever new wind is blowing. And they may be right. It's not my purpose here to settle that dispute. But what I will say is this: the day is coming where speaking of creation may necessarily entail a working knowledge of simulation language and its underlying anxieties in order to make sense to new generations who have never read a Bible, but who have found in simulationism a kind of balm for their existential hauntings.

Which means, at the very least, we should join the conversation now. Listen deeply. Learn humbly. And adapt accordingly. Because what we cannot afford to do is continue speaking of creation within the containers of 1920's liberal vs conservative/ creation vs evolution wars.

Those ships have sailed.

I'll close this chapter like this: I don't have the all answers. It's too soon to tell. Simulation theory may very well flop. But the notion that we are headed toward a redefining of what it means to be spiritual and religious will not. Whether it be simulation spiritualities or religions built around artificial intelligence and digital immortality – something is coming. As Carl Teichrib contends in his book, "Game of God's: The Temple of Man in the Age of Re-Enchantment",

> "The history of Man 'playing God' is one of deepest subjugation and destruction."

And it's making a comeback.

# NOTES

[1]   Thomas, Mike. "What Is Simulation Theory? Are We Living in a Computer Simulation?" Built In, (https://builtin.com/hardware/simulation-theory).

[2]   See Taylor, C. (2007). A Secular Age. Harvard University Press.

[3]   James, Nic. "The Simulation Theory: Bridging Science and Spirituality." Medium, 5 Jan. 2024, (medium.com).

[4]   Visagie, Morné. "A Religion for Atheists: How the Simulation Hypothesis and Multiverse Theories Rely on Faith Rather Than Evidence." Medium, 27 Jan. 2023, (medium.com).

[5]   ibid.

[6]   Orf, Darren. "A Scientist Says He Has the Evidence That We Live in a Simulation." Popular Mechanics, 24 Apr. 2024, (popularmechanics.com)

[7]   Hossenfelder, Sabine. "The Simulation Hypothesis is Pseudoscience." Backreaction, 13 Feb. 2021, (blogspot.com).

[8]   Powell, Corey S. "Elon Musk says we may live in a simulation. Here's how we might tell if he's right." NBC News, 3 Oct. 2018, (nbcnews.com).

[9]   "Neil deGrasse Tyson Explains the Simulation Hypothesis." StarTalk, YouTube, 18 Mar. 2020.

[10] Diamond, Dominik. "If life is one giant computer simulation, God is a rubbish player." The Guardian, 29 Mar. 2024, (theguardian.com).

CHAPTER 12:

# HUMANITY

*"I maintain that faith in this world is perfectly possible without faith in another world."*

**–Rosalind Franklin**

In her poem "Back to Being Human" the English poet Ms. Moem invites us to collectively regress "back" to something we have "lost" about ourselves—a thing that purportedly encapsulates all that it means to be who we are meant to be. But as art would have it, the poem itself does not answer or explain what being human means. Instead, it hints at "complexity" and "harmony" while asking, "What does that mean to you?"[1]

However, I would contend that part of the reason humanity has lost its humanity is precisely because no one really knows what humanity is. On the one hand, philosopher Martha C. Nussbaum posits that the very question "what does it mean to be human?" is narcissistic and ought to be discarded.[2] On the other hand, disgraced apologist Ravi Zacharias contended that to be human means to be "made in the image of God for the glorious reality of being in permanent fellowship with him,"[3] a perspective he did not apply consistently in his own life, throwing its existential validity into doubt. And then, of course, there is the Solipsism philosophical school which maintains that the external world may in fact not exist at all as the only thing we can truly know to exist is our own mind, [4] a contention French philosopher René Descartes famously espoused with his timeless words, "I think, therefore I am."

As surprisingly difficult as it may be to dissect the pillars of human existence, Descartes' contention is rooted in the idea that the very experience of consciousness provides us with a starting point that cannot be doubted because "to doubt implies a doubter"[5] which, as is plainly obvious, presupposes an existence. Existentialists then enter the scene, and with the help of the humanist, construct a new vision of humanity and what it means to be human. But, perhaps most compellingly, the question "what does it mean to be human?" is itself a product of what it means to be human. That is, *it is a question,* and as such, it carries within itself a partial answer to its own inquiry.

Humans, unlike the animal kingdom, ask questions. The capacity for such profound reflection and curiosity is itself a part of what it means to be human. To date, the only animal to ever ask a question was Alex, the parrot who asked "what color?" when looking at himself in a mirror—a question that some psychologists have skeptically interpreted as irrational to the creature itself and which, in the best case scenario, emerged only after decades of psychological experiments.[6]

Thus, it remains clear that one of the central things that separates man from the animal kingdom is the capacity to inquire and investigate—both outflows of possessing consciousness of self, or as American psychologist Rollo May put it in his book "Man's Search for Himself"—"the birth of the human animal into a person"[7]—a thing that can either be perceived as a blessing or, as the poet Walt Whitman decried, a curse for which he envied the animals who, "do not lie awake in the dark and weep for their sins." [8]

We will return to this perspective of consciousness and questions in the next chapter. Nevertheless, beyond the biblical world, what it means to be human is a puzzle that continues to elude any real answer. Practically speaking, this translates into a contemporary secular age in which the question of our humanity is contended with in sporadic chunks with no real cohesion. Many, as already mentioned in previous chapters, have found a degree of contentment in their amusements, duties, and ideologies that protect them from the "need to define."

Add to this the privileged status of most western secularists, who enjoy a level of prosperity and economic security unmatched in the world, and you have the makings of a culture that doesn't feel the need to constantly engage in questions of mortality or humanity. However, this does not mean that the question does not plague them. The navigation systems are only good to the degree that they remain uninterrupted. However, once addiction, divorce, betrayal, depression, or economic catastrophe touches a person's life, their navigation system becomes untenable. As it collapses, most people find themselves unable to cope with the calamity of life they have never had to confront. Perhaps this is one reason why research has found "a higher prevalence of anxiety in wealthier economies"[9] as well as a higher prevalence of depression despite our "globalization of happiness."[10]

So then, as we move forward in our exploration of the secular mind with the aim of reimagining our message and maximizing our evangelistic potential, the next question that must be explored is—how do we engage the secular mind with a meaningful view of humanity in its moments of self-reflection? As usual, it turns out that understanding the ways in which the contemporary mind perceives and relates to the concept of self and humanity is vital if we wish to connect meaningfully with them.

Without oversimplifying to the point of misrepresentation, allow me to summarize the most common approaches to the nature of man we are bound to encounter in the secular world and contrast them with the classic evangelical approach. These approaches are the nihilist, humanist, and postmodern approaches.

## Nihilism, Humanism, and Postmodernism

The modernist approach to the nature of man cannot be separated from the naturalist/ evolutionary approach, which sees man as the result of long ages of cosmic "accidents." In this naturalist view, mankind is essentially a highly developed primate or, as the late theoretical physicist Stephen Hawking put it, "an advanced breed of monkeys on a minor planet with a very average star."[11] There is no metaphysical reason for our existence. We are simply here by accident.

In addition, the universe that we now inhabit will eventually end, and we will cease to exist—a proposition that BBC contributor Adam Becker plays lightly with as he opens his article, "How will the Universe End and Will Anything Survive?" with the statement, "Don't panic, but our planet is doomed."[12] In this eschatological vision, all memory that we were ever here will be erased and if any other life forms evolve in the future, they would have zero inkling that we were ever here or that our universe—let alone our planet—even existed.

This view of humanity leads to two different outcomes. The nihilist sees this as evidence that nothing matters. There is no meaning to existence whatsoever, and the best we can hope to do is live a life that maximizes pleasure while minimizing pain. This means living a balanced life, sensible, and civil. In this sense, we can live a life of maximum potential, enjoy our existence as maximally as possible, and then die and be forgotten. In the end, according to the nihilist, nothing mattered and no one mattered. Life is just a big cosmic joke or, as Alan Moore put it—"a successful virus clinging to a speck of mud suspended in endless nothing."[13]

In fact, in this nihilistic vision, it is even difficult to speak of our existence as an accident. Accidents presuppose intentionality, but in evolution, there is no intention. This means that we are not an accident but are, in fact, less than an accident—the sum of all that is nothingness. Thus, we are nothing and life is nothing. This does not mean we throw all restraint away, because a life without restraint is a life that maximizes pain and minimizes pleasure. Therefore, we strive for civility to avoid crafting misery out of our already meaningless and miserable existence—what Arthur C. Clarke referred to as a "relentless crushing of life and spirit."[14]

The humanist approach differs from the nihilist. The humanist approach is also rooted in the naturalist/evolutionist narrative, but it maintains that although man has no reason for existence, consciousness now affords us the opportunity to create our own meaning. Hawking aimed at this when, after referring to humanity as advanced monkeys, he concluded by adding: "But we can understand the universe. That makes us something very special." Thus, with consciousness as our starting point, we can self-define and self-determine our value and existence. While we may be nothing more than further evolved primates, that evolutionary furtherance enables human capabilities like performing calculus, engineering technological marvels, and composing poetry. This, the humanist, sees as possessing a kind of beauty that must be explored, unearthed, and celebrated. We do not need a God to give us value, we give ourselves value. That is, despite the meaninglessness, we construct meaning nonetheless. In light of this, the humanist Rosalind Franklin stated, "I maintain that faith in this world is perfectly possible without faith in another world."[15]

The postmodernist approach is the final one we will explore, although much more can be written here. The postmodernist approach is similar to the humanist approach, with one major distinction. While the humanist approach tends to view the construction of meaning as a communal act, the postmodern approach views it as an individual act. That is, I construct my own meaning for my own self for "what's right for you may not be right for me"—a perspective Jonathan Merritt defines as once "en vogue" though it is rapidly becoming a "relic."[16] Regardless, this perspective is an essential denial of absolutes and universals. Any objective narrative that attempts to tie the human story together in grand themes is seen as oppressive, or at least, the source of all oppression. In this sense, postmodernism is about the multiplicity of a simultaneity of truths.

As mentioned above, I do not wish to caricature any of these systems of thought. Nihilism, humanism, and postmodernism are, in fact, significantly more complex than what I have presented here. However, I am not aiming to present the academic expression of these ideas, but rather the approaches adopted by the everyday non-philosophical person wandering the isles of the local supermarket. At this pop-cultural level, the above systems do in fact express themselves in less nuanced forms and often adopt a simplistic application to life. Thus, while no postmodern philosopher would ever accept such a bland relativistic approach in terms of what constitutes epistemology, you will find that this approach forms the ethic of many a pop-postmodernist. The same applies to nihilism and humanism.

Before we dive into how these systems interact with the classic evangelical approach, we must first explore what that approach entails to some degree. From there, we will be better prepared to see how worldviews clash and what we can do to close those gaps and connect more meaningfully with the secular world around us.

## Evangelicalism

The most popular perspective of the nature of man in Christianity is essentially this—man is depraved, sinful, fallen, and lost. This perspective does not simply reside in Calvinist churches, but is quite common in conservative Adventism. In essence, Christianity has nothing but bad news regarding human nature. Mankind is filthy, rotten, and corrupt to the core. There is nothing good in us; thus, contemporary Christian musician Ronnie Freeman could sing, "The only thing that's good in me is Jesus."[17]

In this vision of human nature, mankind is, as reformer John Calvin put it, "a five-foot worm"[18]—a sentiment echoed by Isaac Watts in his hymn "Alas, and Did my Savior Bleed?" when he wrote,

"Would He devote that sacred head for such a worm as I?"[19] In this popular evangelical view, any attempts at developing self-esteem or self-value are decried as humanistic deceptions. It appears to many that Christianity, as a faith, cannot be properly embraced without the acceptance of total human depravity, because this depravity is what paves the way for our complete and total dependence on Jesus as our Savior. Without that depravity, many Christians feel that we cannot truly appreciate the sacrifice of Jesus on our behalf. Thus, the most influential evangelical view of human nature is just that— one that emphasizes our complete and total filth and sinful nature in an attempt to deconstruct any sense of self-trust.

A cursory reading of this approach automatically reveals the pitfalls and obstacles it creates in relation to the secular language of being. The classic evangelical view is essentially a metaphysical nihilism that says, "Yes, you are meaningless." But tempered with the sales pitch: "Jesus can give you meaning!" It presents a cynical vision of human nature, one with which a postmodernist might agree according to their dystopian vision of social regression, but which they will nevertheless reject because of the way, it attempts to profit from the human condition to bolster its religious assumptions. Finally, this vision of the human spirit is one which the humanist finds repulsive—a pathological and neurotic pessimism about the very thing that—against all odds—has risen to the height of royalty in a universe that seems to plot our annihilation.

Of course, this is not to say that we ought to soften or change our theology merely to placate modern sensibilities or theories. But it does force us to ask—are we missing something? Is there any sense in which scripture provides us with an approach to the nature of man that is a bit more enthusiastic and hopeful and that can, to some degree, interact meaningfully with the self-affirming priorities of the secular mind?

The answer is yes, and it is found in the Imago Dei, which in turn opens the door to two perspectives, which I refer to as "the limitlessness of man" and "eternal potentiality." Now that we have established our foundation, we will explore these perspectives in the next chapter.

# NOTES

[1]  Ms. Oem, "Back to Being Human."

[2]  Martha C. Nussbaum, "What Does It Mean to Be Human? Don't Ask."

[3]  Ravi Zacharias, "Sermon Quotes: The Image of God."

[4]  The Editors of Encyclopaedia Britannica, "Solipsism."

[5]  Robert G. Brown, "Why Solipsism is Bullshit."

[6]  Tijana Radeska, "Alex the parrot is the only non-human to ask the existential question-'What color am I?'"

[7]  Rollo May, Man's Search for Himself, p. 58.

[8]  Walt Whitman, "Song of Myself," 32.

[9]  Tim Newman, "Anxiety in the West: Is it on the rise?"

[10] Brock Bastian, "Is Our Western Happiness Fetish Causing Depression?"

[11] Miriam Kramer, "This poignant quote from Stephen Hawking sums up his life."

[12] Adam Becker, "How will the Universe End and Will Anything Survive?"

[13] Alan Moore, Watchmen [As quoted in Brad Alles, "Why are we here?"]

[14] Arthur C. Clarke and Stephen Baxter, The Light of Other Days, p. 78.

[15] Rosalind Franklin, letter to her father (summer 1940).

[16] Jonathan Merritt, "The Death of Moral Relativism."

[17] Ronnie Freeman, "The Only Thing" [The Only Thing lyrics © Warner Chappell Music, Inc., Universal Music Publishing Group, Capitol Christian Music Group]

[18] Curt Daniel, "The Depth of Depravity."

[19] Isaac Watts, "Alas, and Did My Savior Bleed?"

CHAPTER 13:

# POST-HUMANITY

---

*"We are not beings born totally depraved. We are beings in need of healing."*

**–Jordan Sutton**

In the 2017 sci-fi thriller "Life," a space crew fights to survive an alien creature that is both hostile and seemingly impossible to destroy. As the film reaches its climax, however, the viewer can discern a rising tension between nihilism and humanism. One of the film's characters, exobiologist Hugh Derry, appears to mourn the crew's demise while simultaneously embracing the inevitability of their death as nothing more than a natural part of the lifecycle. "Calvin [the name given to the alien] doesn't hate us," he says, moments before his death, "but he has to kill us in order to survive."

Derry's defeatist perspective is grounded in what is potentially the film's ideological drive, which he concedes saying, "life's very existence requires destruction." During this portion of the film— arguably its most existential segment—the characters speak of the difficulty of watching humans die while, much to the remaining crew's horror, they discover the alien has hidden itself under Derry's trousers, devouring him as he speaks. Derry never warned his friends, almost as if to say, "don't fight the inevitable. It is what it is." Thus, in contrast to the theme of human value, we find a contending motif of human futility.

As the final two of the original seven-man crew face the undeniability of their approaching death, the crew's physician, David, reads a poem that adds to the nihilistic weight of the film:

Good night, room.

Good night, moon.

Good night, cow jumping over the moon.

Good night, light and the red balloon.

Good night, nobody.

The cold temperature of outer-space merges with the cryptic touch of the poem's indifference. Here they are: hunted and devoured by a being with no self-consciousness—just a cell that has morphed into a killing machine, and in the end, none of it seems to matter. However, the tension in the film, heretofore explored, now emerges with even greater force, for in a moment of epiphany, David and his fellow survivor, quarantine officer Miranda North, concoct a plan to prevent the alien from entering earth. A plan that involves self-sacrifice for the continued survival of humanity, which, in varying degrees, the film itself has suggested, has no objective significance. In the end, the alien manages to enter earth and the film ends, leaving the viewer with the possibility that beyond the credits lies a story of the complete annihilation of the human race.

Herein lies the tension in the film, or should I say, its absurdity. A seeming mockery of the value of human life on the one hand and an instinctive struggle to preserve it against all odds on the other. Considering this tension, we are forced to ask—is human life valuable? And if so, why? And in our quest to discover why, we are once again reintroduced to the timeless question—what does it mean to be human? Does it mean anything at all?

It is in the tension created by this very question that I believe authentic Adventist theology provides us with a vision that is both compelling and beautiful. Beginning with the *Imago Dei* and moving into the limitlessness of man and his eternal potentiality, Adventist theology has the capacity to interact with the absurdity of human ontology in a fundamentally meaningful way because it can both interact meaningfully with the cynicism of the nihilist and the enthusiasm of the humanist while contending with the mistaken presuppositions that undergird these secular perspectives.

## The Imago Dei

The concept of the *Imago Dei* is ancient in that it simply refers to the biblical view that mankind is made in the image of God (*tzelem elohim* in Hebrew). However, where we go from there is a matter of debate. In classical evangelical thought, the fall completely obliterated the image of God in man, rendering him so utterly depraved that even God's word, self-disclosure, and Holy Spirit is incapable of turning man from his sin. Thus, the only way men can be saved in this scenario is if God pre-selects those who will be saved and then regenerates them. Once regenerated, man is now capable of responding to God's voice and can to enter into a relationship with him.[1]

Other perspectives have arisen throughout history. Thus, while this view maintains that God saves only the ones he has elected by regenerating them through his grace, another view insists that God does not preselect whom he will save, but he does, in fact, sanctify the souls of those whom he later saves. Those who experience this sanctification are therefore in a place where they can now choose and thus receive justification.

In this view, sanctification precedes and opens the way to justification because God cannot declare holy what is unholy. [2] Then, there is the view that God justifies before he sanctifies, but since man is so depraved and unable to respond to God's justifying grace, God must first awaken the sinner with "prevenient grace" (a grace before grace). This prevenient grace is like a booster shot from heaven that awakens a person long enough to freely choose whether to receive Jesus or not.[3]

And then, of course, there is the view that God simply justifies with no sanctification in view because the truth is—men are so deplorable that they can never hope to be changed. Therefore, God simply declares us righteous and leaves it at that. Sin, in this view, will always have dominion over us, and so we surrender ourselves to its unending regime. God forgave us, and so now, we can go to heaven, and that's all that matters.[4]

Lastly, there is a view that justification is not enough. It might contribute to salvation, but humanity is so corrupt that we must put forth a considerable amount of effort to self-cleanse the soul temple or else, we will have our justification revoked. In this view, man must accomplish the work of perfecting the self in order to be allowed into eternity.[5] This is, once again, rooted in the idea that we are so deplorable that God simply cannot stomach our filth.

Each of these views exists within the Christian world today—many of them in Adventism. They do not always exist in clear lines. Most of the time, church members adopt aspects from each and manufacture a composite view. However, the foundation tends to be the same no matter which view you embrace or what cocktail you create from the diverse positions you interact with. And that view is essentially that mankind is, well . . . indecent, to put it nicely—reprehensibly fetid to be more precise.

Therefore, this view, when presented without nuance or care to a secular world, is itself reprehensible. It has all the hallmarks of an abusive husband who controls his wife by destroying her self-value with mantras like, "no one will love you" or "you are ugly" or "stupid." Controlling, narcissistic spouses are known to use these phrases to exert dominance over their partner by eroding their sense of self-confidence or autonomy. Consequently, the victim finds themselves in a mental cage that they cannot escape. On the one hand, the abuse is unlivable, but on the other hand, where can the victim ever hope to find acceptance if they are truly so undesirable?

This view is also seen with suspicion by a skeptical world fed up with how religion monetizes psychological guilt for its own self-perpetuation. You tell people they are horrible and that their destiny is eternal death, thus creating a deep existential hole in their psyches. A hole which the church is then more than happy to fill. In a sense, the secular world sees Christianity as a manipulative ideology that has created a pathological need in society which it, in turn, promises to resolve. And of course, sooner or later, that resolution will involve money. Is it not surprising that our neighbors want nothing to do with our faith?

A more meaningful place to begin our journey with a secular world is not with fallen human nature in need of redemption but with the image of God inherently ours. Jefferson Bethke refers to this as the beginning of the journey in Genesis 1 instead of Genesis 3.[6] Thus, contrary to the old Baptist approach of "get them real lost so you can get them real saved," the call is to "get them real loved" instead. That is, to offer the culture a vision of humanity that interacts meaningfully with the pillars of nihilism and humanism, but also transcends those ideologies and offers people a real foundation for loving their essential selves in a way that only a biblical worldview can substantiate.

But is such a position justifiable? After all, doesn't the Bible explicitly declare that man is sinful from birth—schemers, immoral, and evil? The answer is undoubtedly yes. But the Bible also declares that we were made in the image of God (Genesis 1:27); that even in our fallen nature we still know "how to give good" (Matthew 7:11); that we are fearfully and wonderfully made, known from our mother's womb (Psalms 139:13-14); that God delights in us and sings over us (Zephaniah 3:17); and that we are loved—so loved, in fact, that God would give his only son for our redemption (John 3:16), not when we got our act together but in the very midst of our darkest days (Romans 5:8). In the midst of our fallenness, God declares our limitlessness when he says, "nothing that they propose to do will now be impossible" (Genesis 11:6). And of mankind it is said that God is "mindful" of us, has "crowned" us (Psalms 8:4), and has given the earth to us to rule (Psalms 115:16).

It appears that, from the narrative of scripture, there is something about us that is inherently beautiful, valuable, and redemptive. Thus, pastor Jordan Sutton stated, "We are not beings born totally depraved. We are beings in need of healing."[7]

The difference, according to Sutton, is that a "self-deprecating theological position" can lead people to believe that any true metamorphosis of being is "virtually meaningless." Consequently, they go "on and on about how bad they are" instead of the "great work" God has done and is doing. Sutton goes on to mourn how such a low view of man also leads us to forget that "the power of God's eternal act will transform everything about our lives and this world" and that all this is possible because, rather than being contemptible creatures, we are beckoned in Christ to our "original goodness."

Scripture beautifully captures this vision, of our value, by comparing us to a pearl of great worth buried in a field (Matthew 13:45-46), for which God gave everything to acquire. Or as wandering children coming home—not to a disgusted reception, but to a father longing to have us with him (Luke 15:11-32). For every person who returns, the Bible says there is a feast in heaven (Luke 15:10), and when Jesus came to earth, it was not the religious whose presence he enjoyed, but the outcasts and misfits (Matthew 9:11). And the gospel of the kingdom he entrusted to the church, not angels (1 Peter 1:12)—an act that speaks highly of God's respect for man.

None of this denies the reality of man's fallen nature and our inability to save ourselves. But what it does is invite the secular seeker into a narrative that interacts meaningfully with their language of being—particularly the heroic vision of man and its inherent appreciation of autonomy, self-determination, and affirmation—

all while prodding at the false assumptions of humanism and its altogether exaggerated anthro-enthusiasm that sees mankind as essentially good, or neutral at best.

Thus, the Biblical narrative–especially as understood by Adventism–does not see man as a "worm" in any ontological sense, but rather, as royalty created in the image of God–an image that sin will never obliterate. We are fallen, yes, we are incapable of self-redemption, yes. But we are not loathsome. There is something beautiful about us–not so much within or in our possession–but essentially us.

To put it simply, there is not a thing "within" man that is to be considered valuable; rather, man, in his total self, is the valuable thing. When we begin the story there, in Genesis 1, we naturally unfold a different kind of narrative where, rather than starting at how bad we are so we can convince people of how much they need salvation, we begin at how incredibly gorgeous we are in order to awaken within our audience the very real call that they were made for more than this world and its amusements, duties, and ideologies can ever offer.

## The Limitlessness of Man and His Eternal Potentiality

From this enthusiastic starting place, Adventists can then interact more convincingly with reality. A phrase, I have often heard in traditional Adventist churches is that "man, without the Spirit of God, can do nothing good." There is, of course, theological accuracy to this. However, people don't often use those words with their inherent theological nuance; rather, they use them as a means to attack and demonize culture. In this sense, the phrase becomes a way of saying that *unless you belong to my church and believe as I do, you cannot do good in the world, and even if you are a nice and ethical person, you are still evil.*

The problem with this view is that it is both uninformed and entirely outlandish to the secular mind. A brief look at history shows that mankind is certainly capable of immense good even without faith in Jesus. To a secular world reeling from the scandals of child abuse within the church itself, the proposition that one must belong to the church and be a Christian to produce tangible good is insulting.

While far from perfect (a quality that non-religious individuals may not embrace), most people today admire figures like the Hindu Mohandas Gandhi, Muslim Malala Yousafzai, and the Buddhist Dalai Lama as pragmatic examples of human goodness. In his news report "The Joy of Giving," wealthy chef turned social worker, Narayanan Krishnan speaks of how he turned his back on his own religious identity in order to serve the needs of the outcast, rejected, and despised people of India. Krishnan is, himself, not a follower of Jesus and yet exemplifies the spirit of giving in a way that puts most Christians to shame.

None of these people are perfect, of course, but the culture regards them as inspiring and real—not the photoshopped (and phony) version of saintliness that the church often portrays. And when I look at scripture, I don't find this a difficult notion to appreciate. Not only did Jesus speak highly of the faith of a pagan centurion (in fact, he said his faith was greater than all of Israel), but scripture itself strongly alludes to man's limitlessness and eternal potential for self-advancement in the very doctrine of worship itself.

Recall from the articles on God and absurdity that an important element to maintain when exploring God in the secular world is his differentiation. That is, God approves of himself, glorifies himself, and exalts himself. He does not need us to feed his ego or stroke his sense of self-importance. This naturally leaves us with a question— what, then, is the objective of worship? The reason for this tension is that we are used to thinking of worship as something we do for God. However, what if worship was something God does for us?

Many years ago, I noticed a secular contact struggling with the idea of worshiping God or having to depend on God for anything. The whole thing just seemed unfair. To navigate the experience with him, I shared what psychiatrist Timothy Jennings had referred to in one of his talks as the "other-centered motive of worship." In this sense, worship is not a divine ego trip; rather, it is an act of other-centeredness. From there, I challenged my contact by asking him *what makes God, GOD?* Among the answers, there emerged this idea that God is inherently self-existing. That is, he does not derive his existence from anything. I then asked him, "Can God create another God?"

We eventually agreed—no, he cannot. For if God is inherently self-existing, the moment God creates another "God," that being is by nature *not* self-existing. If he were, he would not need to be created. Therefore, we concluded that a created being simply cannot be God.

Because mankind is created, this means he is not self-existent, which means he necessarily derives his existence. As a result, man can never be God, because God's existence is inherently non-derivative. Thus, the moment God creates, the created being is by definition not God and neither can he ever be. In order to be God, your essential self must be underived. Thus, there can only be one

God, and all created beings are, in their very reality, a derived life. However, if you are a derived life and not a non-derived life, that means you derive your life from a source that provides you with that life. And if that source, which we know to be God, created you out of love (which we saw in the Trinity and Absurdity), then it logically follows that God wants you to grow, advance, and evolve.

But how can a man grow, advance and evolve? The only way to do this is if he sets his eyes on the non-derived essence from which he derives his being and invests his eternal existence in pursuit of relationship with that essence. Because man is a derivative life form, he will naturally seek to derive meaning and transcendence from somewhere. It's a part of our reality.

On the other hand, if we turn to an animal, an experience, a chemical, another human, or an inanimate object as the god we worship, we stunt our development of being. The reason is simple—we were created to advance into limitless and eternal potential because that's what God is. We might never be God ourselves, but our developmental capacity is infinite. However, that capacity is stunted if the object of our worship is either less than us (an animal, chemical, experience, or object) or equal to us (another human being). Even spiritual beings like angels do not qualify for worship, for scripture tells us that we have been crowned higher than them.

This means that if you want to advance to the fullest level of human development, it can only be done if the object of your highest admiration is God himself. With our psyche locked into his, we become more human. With our worship of anything else, we become less so. Thus, God declares that he will not share his worship with another because he is a jealous God—not jealous for himself as some needy boyfriend, but jealous on our behalf like a mother who wants her daughter to reach the stars and resents anyone's efforts to dissuade her from her noble birthright.

In short, the biblical vision of man holds a tension between two simultaneous realities. The first is our *Imago Dei,* which carries with it the weight of our infinite potentiality and the limitlessness for which we were created. The second concept is the fallen nature of humanity, which, far from denying our inherent value, amplifies it. Sin is an intruder, a virus that limits our species and robs us of our infinite potential by incarcerating us in the limited cages of trauma, pathology, and vacuous modes of being. Salvation is not God saying, "You are a worm but if you believe in me, I will save you," but rather, a song from heaven that celebrates our *Imago Dei* and invites us to believe that in Jesus, sin has been defeated, the limitations have been shattered, the chains of addiction broken, the prison of fear crushed, the sting of death reversed, and we can once again, through trust in Christ's finished work, taste the grandeur and magnificence for which we were birthed.

## The Posthuman Tension

Interestingly, the tension found between man's fallenness and royalness is also found in the posthuman project. Unlike classical humanism which posited that man was either inherently good or a blank slate upon birth, posthumanism embraces both mans inherent virtue as well as our ontological limitations and failures.

The solution to this tension is where posthumanism really shines. By blending man with machine, we take control of the process of evolution and transcend ourselves into a higher and more advanced form. Gene editing will allow us to edit out the bad genes that cause disease and even mental illness,[8] and by blending man with AI, we can enhance our intelligence to such incredible heights that no problem would be too complex for us to solve. The technological advancements we could achieve in this post-human state would be beyond anything we thought possible, including (but not limited to) telekinetic communication and digital immortality.[9]

In short, mankind is still trying to save itself. Only our redemptive quest is no longer religious, it is now secular and driven by quantum mechanics, AI, and Silicon Valley.

But this is good news, because it shows that the worldview is shifting back from a "we don't need a savior" mentality. While the savior being proposed is far from the God of scripture, the door is once again opening to the conversation over mankind's need of redemption. A conversation which we, as Adventists, can engage meaningfully with a theology of man that embraces our limitless potential and our fallen realty at the same time.

### Summary: The Supreme Value of Man

To summarize, a more meaningful approach to human nature as it relates to secular outreach is one that embraces the tension between the very real fallenness of man while simultaneously celebrating what Ellen White referred to as the "beautiful chambers"[10] of the human mind. We are broken and bent to evil, yes. Nevertheless, we remain "the noblest of His created works"[11] and the objects of his supreme desire, whom he looks upon with "unutterable longing."[12]

These truths, White, viewed as foundational to what she referred to as "respect for the dignity of man as man"[13]—a view grounded in the "precious material"[14] that make up who we are. Best of all, White writes that in Christ we are "not degraded, but raised, ennobled, refined…"[15] Thus, White contends that "it is not pleasing to God that [we] should demerit [ourselves]."[16] On the contrary, we must "cultivate self-respect."[17] These two perspectives–the fallenness of man and the nobility of man–must be held in tension and carefully presented when interacting with a culture that is either steeped in a cynical vision of man's futility, or the false enthusiasm of innate human virtue.

As we conclude this segment on the nature of man and absurdity, my encouragement to Adventists everywhere, particularly preachers and evangelists, is to reject the classical evangelical view of human depravity. Not only is it unbiblical, but it is also highly pathological and fails to interact with the secular language of being. A better approach is to celebrate the beauty of the human spirit and its moments of historical grandeur, while holding space for our fallenness. Indeed, if we are ever to attain our maximal potential in both individual and collective expression, we simply need to reconnect to the source of our being. In doing so, eternity will afford us a progression so infinite that our imaginations can scarcely grasp its magnificence.

# NOTES

[1]  The view expressed here is the Calvinist/Reformed view.

[2]  The view expressed here is a summary of the Jesuit perspective on prevenient grace.

[3]  The view expressed here is the classical Arminian and Wesleyan view on prevenient grace.

[4]  The view expressed here is commonly known as once-saved-always-saved, or the doctrine of "eternal security."

[5]  The view expressed here is known within Adventism as last generation theology.

[6]  Jefferson Bethke, as quoted in "Challenging Your Christianity."

[7]  Jordan Sutton, "Are We Good or Evil? The Problem with Total Depravity."

[8]  Steinmark, Ida Emilie. "Does gene editing hold the key to improving mental health?" The Guardian, 26 Feb. 2023, (theguardian.com).

[9]  "Neuralink's Brain Chip: How It Works and What It Means." Capitol Technology University, 9 Feb. 2024, (captechu.edu).

[10] Ellen G. White, Testimonies, vol. 6, p. 375.

[11] Ellen G. White, Faith I Live By, p. 29.

[12] Ellen G. White, The Desire of Ages, p. 517.

[13] Ellen G. White, Mind, Character, and Personality, vol. 1, p. 255.

[14] Ibid.

[15] Ellen G. White, Selected Messages, vol. 3, p. 135.

[16] Ellen G. White, Mind, Character, and Personality, vol. 1, p. 260.

[17] Ibid.

# CONCLUSION

In Volume 1 of Adventism+ I have attempted to lay a foundation for mission in our metamodern present with a vision for our rapidly advancing post-human era. And we have done so primarily in three areas of Adventist belief: Our doctrines of God, Creation, and Man (contained within fundamental beliefs 1-7).

On the doctrine of God, I contend that a move away from "attributes" and "claims", replacing these with perspectives that focus more on God's "inherence" and "virtue" are not only more biblical, but more missional. Not to mention, posthumanisms vision for AI may very well open the door to a whole new set of religions and spiritualities in which the deity is known primarily through attributes and claims. A picture of God grounded in inherence and virtue is not only more biblical, it is also more relevant and anticonformist in a world where the very concept of deity undergoes a radical revisioning.

We also spoke about creation and the need to step away from the classical creation vs evolution squabbles of the modernist era, instead aiming to promote a more existential and healing picture of creation that addresses the anxieties of the age (emerging secular culture is no longer anxious about whether or not we come from monkeys or God) as well as those to come (as seen through the popularization of the Simulation hypothesis).

Finally, we explored the nature of man and the need for Adventism to resist classical evangelical anthropologies that de-humanize and de-value mankind while maintaining a balance that emphasizes our complete and total need for a savior. This balance is already present in the posthuman project which seeks to upgrade humanity to a higher state of being via the blending of man with machine. For the Christian this task has already been accomplished in Jesus, who "upgraded" our species through the blending of "man with divinity" (more to come in Vol 2).

However, each of these doctrinal rearticulations emerge from primordial shifts in our theological pressupostions. These shifts, I contend, must involve a move away from fundamentalism's "static truth" mood, and back to Adventisms radical "flow truth" perspective. Not only is this perspective more faithful to the text, it interacts more meaningfully with secularisms language of being and its disenchanted contention with absurdity.

As we progress, we will broaden our contextualization by diving into fundamental beliefs 8-11 which explore the Great Controversy and the Gospel. We will continue to revisit the foundations laid in this volume as we anchor ourselves in the existential hauntings that undergird our metamodern age and the post-human era to come.

Until then,

Here's to an Adventism. Redesigned.

Pastor Marcos | The Story Church Project

> If you are a missional Adventist with
> a passion for secular mission....

# I WANT TO INVITE YOU TO JOIN MY ONLINE INNOVATIVE MISSION ACADEMY

Explore secular mission and contextualization with LIVE sessions, a GLOBAL community of missional SDA's, and over 30 hours of video workshops covering RELEVANT topics like posthumanism, metamodernism, postmodernism and more.

Go to: www.thestorychurchproject.com/TMC

Made in United States
Orlando, FL
30 November 2024

54673265R00104